Don't Miss School on Mondays!

Stories for Teachers Who Love to Teach

Pat James

PRISTINE
PRESS AND MEDIA

ISBN
978-1-969642-03-6 (Paperback)
978-1-969642-02-9 (eBook)
978-1-969642-04-3 (Hardcover)

Dedication

One of my first grade students told his mother, *"I have to go to school on Monday; Mrs. James misses us too much on the weekend."* This book is dedicated to all of the students who came back for me every Monday. Your presence in my class gave me so much joy – and very white hair!

This book is also dedicated to the *"weekend children"* in my life – my Sunday School students in Indiana, California, Washington and Texas and to my faithful co-teacher, my amazing husband Jerry.

God bless you, Sweeties,
Mrs. James or Grannie or Pat

Contents

Introduction

This book is written to encourage! Teaching is a difficult profession, and it is becoming increasingly challenging. But there are those individuals in teaching who feel called of God to teach, who revel in the assignment, and who, against all odds, meet the challenge. My prayer is that those teachers will not *"become weary in doing good for at the proper time we will reap a harvest if we do not give up." Galatians 6:9* It is also my prayer that those teachers will, in turn, be encouragers of those around them.

In this book there are 36 Monday messages for the 36 Mondays of the traditional school year. Each story is accompanied by a required reading - a scripture to lift you up as you do your most important job M-F. And, in the best teaching practice, there will be homework - a teaching idea or tip.

After writing my first book, *I Love Monday Mornings,* I was touched by the number of teachers who responded, through laughter and tears, to the stories. One former colleague wrote, "I feel like a young college girl I once was with all my first visions of what education should be." This book is written for all teachers, young and old, who hold to a positive philosophy of our great profession.

In humility, remembering that "Teacher" was one of the titles ascribed to our Lord and Savior Jesus Christ,

Pat James

Let's get started!

Required reading: *I urge you to live a life worthy of the calling you have received. Be completely humble and gentle; be patient, bearing with one another in love. Ephesians 4:1b, 2**

Homework: Read this book!

*All scriptures are from the New International Version, published by Tyndale House Publishers, Inc., Wheaton, IL and Zondervan Publishing House, Grand Rapids, MI.

August/September

Measuring Students

In the late seventies, it was a common practice to place children, even primary children, into ability groups. Our school dropped this in preference to heterogeneous grouping after seeing how very hard it is to judge the true ability of the very young. I remember teaching a group of students in the third group from the top of seven language arts groups, based on their readiness tests. In twelve short years one of these so-called "high-average" students was named one of the top ten scholars in the entire city of San Antonio. How glad I am that she was unaware of our "labeling" and didn't know she was not the best! Another year I was assigned the fourth out of seven language arts groups. As my homeroom students were lining up to go to the cafeteria, a big discussion transpired as to which teacher had the best group. Finally, to put an end to the argument, a child asked me, "Who has the best language arts class?" I fumbled for an explanation that would not name groups. One of my homeroom boys who was also in my little class of "low average" children smiled at me and said, "We do, don't we, Mrs. James?" I smiled back, thinking to myself, "If you are doing your very best and working at your own speed, then, yes, you are in the best class - for you."

Thankfully, first graders are generally gracious to those who have lower abilities and generally indifferent to the abilities of those on the other end of the bell-shaped curve. Children who showed signs of giftedness in the early grades were placed in a pull-out program formerly called the "Talent Pool," with extra mental stimulation for them. One day, not seeing my only "gifted" child in the room, I asked the class, "Did Justin have to go to the nurse during PE?"

"No," Isaac explained, "he had to go to that swimming thing."

"Swimming" or "Special," each child is a unique work of art to enjoy. I have found that teachers are actually in the business of edifying – the construction business. I love the word "edify." It's somewhat archaic, coming from the same Latin root word as "edifice," or building. Edify means to build up or strengthen morally. That's our job. We construct self-esteem. Building is hard work, but on the days when we witness children feeling esteemed, we would gladly work for half salary. I experienced some of those days with Stevie, Shirley, and Clint.

When Stevie came to me, he was in his second year of first grade. While I believe in early retention when necessary, my heart goes out to retainees, and I feel a special mission to help them be successful. Stevie did have a moderately good déjà vu year and wrote me from second grade. [sic]

"Did you get any won how was as good as me? I am eslent at math, spelling, science, social studies and English." It helped my own self-esteem to think that I had a part in his thinking that he was the best "won" in my class.

Or consider Shirley, a child without much joy in her young life. She came to us in March after her mother "disappeared" and her grandmother became her guardian. She wrote, [sic]

> "You are nice too me
> She make me happy
> She makes me laughed."

Perhaps the time she was in school was the happiest time of her day.

Clint was the best artist I have ever taught. When he was nearing the end of third grade, he wrote me a treatise on why I might like to move up a few grade levels myself. [sic] "You are my favorite teacher in the whole world. Would you please start teaching fourth grade next year? I want to be in your class again. You said you thought I was 'honerable' at art." Somehow the word "honerable" touched my heart and brought tears to my eyes. I esteemed his art. He was edified.

What a wonderful profession is teaching! We have the express duties as outlined in the state mandates and also the implied benefits of building self-esteem in those so close to the foundation of their lives.

Here is the hard part – while teachers have to evaluate students in order to meet their individual needs, we must fight a constant battle against viewing children only as an alpha or numeric grade, a percentage on an achievement test, or a point on the I.Q. chart. Each child is worthy because of who he is, not because of the scores he can produce or how good he can make us look on evaluations. A song that has come to have more meaning to me as a teacher concerning measuring students is "The Measure of a Man" as sung by 4Him.

> "The world can analyze and size you up and
> throw you on the scales
> They can I.Q. you and run you through their
> rigorous details.
> They can do their best to rate you, and they'll
> place you on the charts
> And then back it up with scientific smarts.
> But there's more to what you're worth
> Than their human eyes can see.
> Oh, I say the measure of a man
> Is not how tall you stand
> How wealthy or intelligent you are
> 'Cause I've found out the measure of a man
> God knows and understands
> For He looks inside to the bottom of your heart.
> And what's in the heart defines
> The measure of a man.

> Written by Mark R. Harris, Donald A. Koch,
> and Stephane Rachel Lewis

Required reading: *Do not be proud, but be willing to associate with people of low position. Do not be conceited. Romans 12:1b*

Then Peter began to speak, *"I now realize how true it is that God does not show favoritism…" Acts 10:34*

When God created man, he made him in the likeness of God. He created them male and female and blessed them. Genesis 5: 1b, 2a

Homework: Find work from a so-called "low average" child today, and use it as your good example for the rest of the class to follow. You will bless this child and edify him. He will think he is the best "won!"

9/11

On September 11, 2001, I was in my classroom teaching 20 children. Both they and I were unaware that the world as we knew it was changing even as we worked on what Matthew called "pluses and takekowase." Our assistant principal slipped into my room and told me not to turn on the TV. Since I hadn't planned to use the TV that morning, I put his words aside and taught the lesson I had planned. About 10 o'clock my husband Jerry appeared at the back of the classroom. I was surprised since he had reservations to fly south to the Texas valley that morning on business. "What's wrong?" I asked him as I walked to the back of the room. "You were supposed to be gone."

"You haven't heard," he said sadly and proceeded to tell me how terrorists had flown into the Twin Towers, the Pentagon, and a third plane had been diverted from the White House. He had been informed of this in the airport as he was starting to board the plane. It was the first time in history that all airports had been closed.

I finished the morning in a state of numbness, thankful that I had not heard the somber news earlier. Lunch was spent around the TV with other teachers as we watched reruns of our country literally being altered as surely as the New York skyline on that fateful day.

Our school made the correct decision to let parents interpret the horrors to their children in their own way. In the afternoon there was a feeble attempt to conduct "business as usual" in the classroom. Still unsure of the breadth of the terror attacks as school ended, we all walked the children to their cars at 2:45. I stood with a lump in my throat and felt almost detached from the after-school goodbyes. I kept thinking sadly, "They will never know the world that I have known."

Fear of flying was rampant in the days following 9/11. I had reservations to fly to California to see one of my granddaughters in a community theatre production just nine days after the attack. I wrestled with the decision to stay or to go. I chose to go. I entered the eerily quiet San Antonio airport. The normal hubbub was changed to silent apprehension. Strangers were sizing others up as to the possibility of their being terrorists. I felt their eyes on me even as I checked them out. My eyes stopped on a man in a turban. He was accompanied by what looked like a wife and two small children. "Surely, he wouldn't…" I reasoned, "not with a family." Then I worried that this could be a ploy, and a real terrorist would not care if he took his family down with him.

Just as I was thinking, "I hope that man isn't on my flight," I realized what was happening in my own heart. Almost instantly after the attack there had been a change in the way people in this country related to people of Middle Eastern descent. I had let my prejudice grow, pure and simple, based on a turban and nationality. It was a prejudice I would have to confront soon on a personal level.

In November in the teachers' lounge, I overheard a fifth grade teacher telling about a Muslim girl in her class who was celebrating the Fast of Ramadan. Almost all Muslims over the age of 12 are required to "abstain from food, drink, and other sensual pleasures" from dawn until sunset. According to the Qur'an, Zia was not required to observed the noon fast, but she chose to abstain. "So what does she do during lunchtime?" I asked.

"She sits with the class, but she does not eat."

Knowing from my own on-again, off-again diets how difficult that would be, I asked, "Is your lunch at a time that Zia could come to my class to help?" It was, and every day during the celebration of Ramadan, Zia came. She read to children. She read with children. She graded papers. She won our hearts. When the first graders would see her in the halls, it was like a celebrity sighting.

In November Zia helped nip the root of prejudice that had started to grow on 9/11. While I believe strongly that there is only one way to God, I also know that Jesus, who is The Way, said to love our neighbors as ourselves.

Required reading: *Jesus answered, "I am the way and the truth, and the life. No one comes to the Father except through me." John 14:6*

"Of all the commandments, which is the most important?" "The most important one," answered Jesus, "is this: 'Hear, O Israel, the Lord our God, the Lord is one. Love the Lord your God with all your heart and with all your soul and with all your mind and with all your strength.'

The second is this: 'Love your neighbor as yourself.' There is no commandment greater than these." Mark 12:28b-31

Homework: Pick a minority student for a helper. The love and admiration of your class could make a real difference in the life of this child.

Teachers Don't Have Customers

I taught for a while next door to the teacher of children identified as gifted. And the teacher, my friend Gail, was gifted herself. She had to be to keep up with the challenge of scheduling a pull-out program. Her classes were on a totally different time schedule from our first grade. Unfortunately for her, the sinks for washing hands were in her room.

One day I sent Kristina over to see if she had a class at that moment or if that might be a good time to wash our hands for lunch. Kristina peeked into the room and hurried back to me. "No, she's got a customer," she reported.

What a unique school it would be if students were indeed customers! Imagine the exchange with them.

"May I help you?"

"Yes, I'd like some digraphs to help in my reading."

"Sure, right over here. We have some lovely and useful ones – sh, ch, th, and wh. Which one were you interested in?"

The problem with this paradigm is that many of our customers don't even know what kind of help they need. It is up to the teacher to create a need, fill it, and guarantee to be there in case of product failure or user forgetfulness. That is why teaching is considered an "art," not a "science." No two students learn in exactly the same way. One may need drama while another may need only to be told. One may need to see it on paper while all of them seem to be kinesthetic in first grade. So the teacher puts out the "products" in as many ways as possible to reach the unique modality of each student. I'm always amused at the suggestion for the teacher that is on the special education paperwork. It suggests that the teacher may need to use multi-sensory methods for this particular child. And not for the entire class? It is inherent in primary teaching to use all of possible methods to teach. And this goes way beyond the teacher's guide. While the teaching ideas in the guide may be good, it takes a professional, who is personally acquainted with the needs of each student, to determine which methods to use.

Not all people know how creative this process can be. All that some people outside education think that we have to do is to get the teacher's edition, and let the learning begin! In the August 18, 2004, edition of *The Dallas Morning News* this attitude was reportedly unabashedly verbalized by an attorney who was criticizing school funding testimony by Jim Smith, a consultant for Management, Analysis and Planning, a firm that specializes in school finance issues. The attorney, Linda Helper, asked, "What particular expertise do teachers have – teachers who have to teach from textbooks that are mandated by the state of Texas, that have to teach a curriculum that's mandated by the [state] - what particular expertise do teachers have in designing educational instructional programs?"

Mr. Smith rebutted this "customer" mentality of teaching, saying, "I think it's unfair to characterize their job as just robots that just speak what the state tells them to speak. That's not what goes on in schools."

Unfortunately, it's not just those outside education who have the idea that all it takes to teach are textbooks and a state curriculum. I recently talked to an educator in a neighboring state who told me that all of the physics teachers in that state were required to be on the same page on the same day. And the teachers were monitored to ensure that this was happening! What a bad example of consumer mentality in the guise of progress and accountability.

Maybe educators should "advertise" more so that the public would understand the "art" that is in teaching. And, in one of the commercials, we can tell them that we don't get to pick our clients. They just come, and we just teach them using every imaginable method!

But, in truth, I guess the business paradigm is operating at least in one instance: We will always have the problem with "customers" who are "just looking."

Required reading: *Again crowds of people came to him, and as was his custom, he taught them.*
Mark 10:1

Homework: Try a new method with a difficult spelling word. Use drama! For example, let three children hold the letters A-R-E. Let R come up alone and say, "To write the word 'are,' all you need is me!" Then A and E pop up on either side and say, "Not so fast, buddy, you need us, too." The children love this and will act it out over and over, and you will notice that they will spell the word "are" correctly after this lesson. This would also work on the words "be" and "you" and "tea."

Speech Pwobwems

A new speech therapist had just been hired at our school. She had a very large class load and was trying to get to know each child. She called Angie out of my class for an initial visit. After a few pleasantries, the new teacher asked her, "What sounds were you working on in speech last year, Angie?"

"I don't wemembuh," she answered truthfully. The new teacher had her information!

Sometimes it's not pronunciation that trips children up but homonyms and homophones. Three-year-old Rick was asked in Sunday School what "kind" meant. He replied with a commercial, "McDonald's is your kind of place."

Words start "coming in" at about the same time as teeth in a baby. And big words start "coming in" about the same time as the second set of teeth. Children love big words and like to try out words that adults use, often with humorous takes. Sometimes it's not the oral deficiencies, but the aural, that confuses children. They just hear the words wrong.

Annika was unhappy with her sister for saying, "Oh, Lord!"

"Megan," she chided, "I don't think you're supposed to take the name of the Lord insane!"

Karla, too, had religious word transposition. She was trying to tell me why she would not be at school on Friday. It seems that she was going out of town for a family gathering. But the message I got was, "I'm going to go see my cousin get hypnotized."

"Hypnotized?" I asked.

"Yes, so he won't go, (pointing down.) you know."

I then surmised that the family must have been planning to attend a baptism for a new baby cousin.

Imagine the bewilderment of Sean who went to the YMCA's Prime Time after-school program. He told me that his parents had sent him to "Crime Time."

Children are enamored with secret codes and even teacher codes. Our school had a strange set of codes for "easy" reference teacher-to-teacher. For example K=did not follow directions and X=talking out. One day Eisa breathlessly entered the classroom to report on Andrew's behavior. "Andrew got a W in music." Then in a quieter voice she reasoned, "Wiggling, I guess."

Lyrics to songs we hear on the radio are often muffled and misunderstood by children due to diction of the musician, instrumental interference, or poor-quality radio reception. One child was sure the words to "More Than a Woman" were "Bald-Headed Woman."

Our granddaughter, riding in the back of a crowded van was listening to Elvis Presley's "Jailhouse Rock" for the first time. Suddenly she looked at me in disbelief. "Grannie, did you hear what that man said? He said, 'If you can't find a potty, find a piece of wood or a chair!'"

She relaxed when I cleared up the lyrics, "If you can't find a partner, use a wooden chair. Let's rock!"

I grew up in a church that valued scripture memorization. I credit much of my vocabulary knowledge to extensive training in King James English. Even the very young children learned a verse every week in Sunday School.

One Sunday after we arrived home from church, my parents asked my three-year-old brother Mike to say his memory verse. Proudly Mike quoted, "Serve the Lord with Mama!" He seemed so pleased with himself, but we were all bewildered. While this was a noble thought, we couldn't "chapter and verse" it.

Mom went to the phone and called his teacher Mrs. Green. "What was the memory verse that you taught the children this morning?"

"It was Psalm 100:2 'Serve the Lord with gladness.'"

Slowly, Mom realized the misunderstanding. Her name was "Gladys."

We still laugh at and with Mike over this, but deep down, we know that he was right.

Required reading: *My tongue will tell of your righteous acts all the day long. Psalm 71:24a*

Homework: Help extend vocabulary this week by letting the children think of all of the meanings they can for each of the spelling words. And don't let them use the spelling words in giving their definitions!

October

Compassion

I am always running into things. On the hit TV sitcom "Everybody Loves Raymond," Ray decides in one episode that he should keep a "Bruise Journal" so he could remember how he got discolorations on his body. I really identified with him. I would have entries like: "10/3 Walked too fast into back room and wrapped two smallest toes around folding chair." Usually toe-bumping pain subsides in a few minutes, but this pain did not. The next morning I was unable to put on a shoe over my swollen toes. I hobbled to school wearing only hose on the injured foot.

"What happened?"

"Does it hurt?"

"Oh, no!"

"Ouch!"

I was greeted by a chorus of sympathetic, even empathetic, first graders, each of whom had probably had a toe-bump story. They all wanted to help their maladroit teacher. One would fetch books from my desk. Another would bring me my glasses which I continually forget that I wear. A few even pushed me in the rolling desk chair so my feet did not have to hit the floor. What a great day for love and compassion in our classroom!

I awoke the next morning with the same pain, donned the same stylish sock, and limped into the same group of children. This time I was met with "Are you still hurt?" Compassion was fleeting! I was left to heel-walk around the room and get my own books and glasses all day. I later had the toes x-rayed and found that I had, indeed, broken not one, but two toes. Even that information would not have mattered to the children who were tired of dealing with another's pain.

My high school Latin made me think compassion came from two words meaning "with love." Actually, it comes from two Latin words meaning "feel or suffer together." Everyone needs compassion. Teachers need compassion. Students need compassion. Even the students' parents need compassion. This was made crystal clear to me my first year of teaching first grade.

The school had called an "ARD" (Admission, Review, Dismissal) meeting for a student who had been having learning struggles. To do this, a committee is convened to discuss the best and least restrictive educational program for that individual child. At an "Admission" or "Review," an IEP or Individual Education Program is constructed. That sounds noble. But at my first ARD I saw one person who looked scared and bewildered – the child's mom. The room was filled with school personnel – classroom teacher, speech teacher, reading teacher, principal, nurse, test administrator, district personnel – all speaking in acronyms – ARD, ED, LD, IEP, ADD, ADHD. All of these people were speaking about her child – her baby, only six short years from her womb.

I watched her furtive eyes searching the unfamiliar faces who were telling her about her son. She humbly listened, trying to assimilate all of the terms and information that were new to her. When it came my turn to give my educational assessment of Mark, I found these words tumbling out of my mouth. "I love Mark. We all want the very best for him." Then I launched into his educational needs.

Up to that time I had not really thought about loving this particular child, Mark. Somehow speaking words of love opened the flow of compassion from my own heart. I saw the child in a new light. I have since learned that "speaking love" outloud actually helps love to come for a child.

Required reading: *Filled with compassion, Jesus reached out his hand and touched the man. Mark 1:41a*

Homework: Say it! Think of that child who takes all of your energy or is on your last nerve. Tell someone, "I love that child." Watch the change in yourself and in your attitude toward him. Compassion creates change.

Conference T-I-M-E

It all begins with an 8½ x11" page with a fill-in-the-blanks suggested time for a parent conference. Innocuous enough. But it is received differently in the 20 different homes it enters. Some parents mark the date on the calendar, enter it in a small planner, and reply the very next day as to their intention to be at the conference. These are the parents you don't really need to see. Some parents never see the form or delay answering and lose the paper. Extra form(s) have to be sent. These are the parents you really need to see.

I wonder about parents who aren't curious about the person who will spend approximately 1000 hours with their child. This person will often spend more time with their child that they will during the next 36 weeks, especially if the child attends an after-school program.

The lose-the-form-need-another-one parent often does not show up once the date has been agreed upon. Then the process begins again. I am mildly annoyed if an afternoon appointment fails to show since I generally stay late and have much work to do after school. But not so if a morning appointment defaults! I have my mornings timed down to the minute - wake up, drink coffee, watch TV news, walk two miles, drink second cup of coffee, eat breakfast, read newspaper, shower, dress, drive to school, begin teaching! For an early appointment I have to rearrange my morning. Other professionals charge for missed appointments that have not been canceled 24 hours in advance. School finance issues might be solved if this same policy were put in place! As it is now, teachers just grouse and reschedule.

The week of the first parent-teacher conferences is very emotionally draining. Parents often reveal much about their own lifestyles, as well as their child's home life and the value they assign to that child in these conferences. After one particularly grueling conference, my understanding husband knew my angst and rewarded me with a chicken fried steak dinner, a teddy bear, and a good teacher award!

Conferences have produced some strange visitors to the school. We have had divorced parents who were so cordial to each other that I could not imagine why they split. We have had divorced parents who were not so cordial. I have had a parent come wearing an ankle monitor. I have had a dad who assured me that he was spending time with his children. He said, "I take them with me when I referee football games on the weekends." One of the most humorous was a mom who, upon hearing that her son was struggling academically, asked, "Could this be hereditary? My husband's people are all like that!" She was referred to the counselor to follow up on that technical question.

One common thread runs through conversations with parents. Time. Time really is the great equalizer. Everyone gets exactly the same amount to use. The people who seem to fit so much into their lives are probably good at time management. Many families are experiencing what Dr. James Dobson calls "routine panic" in his book, *Bringing Up Boys*. He explains that people often say, "It's not the quantity, but the quality, of time that matters," as an excuse to give neither to their children. And sometimes we simply get so busy with life that we forget to live.

I have wondered why some people even have children – just to see which relative the baby looks like? Don't they want to spend time with the child, to be there for his first tooth, to hear his first word, to cheer at his first homerun, or to listen to him read his first book? Don't they want to influence his learning, his moral values, his attitudes? Don't they want to "parent?" All of these things require parents to spend hours and hours and hours with a child.

Once I called a dad on the phone to try to make an appointment. He said that he was so busy that it was hard to make time for a conference with me concerning his daughter's grades. He was a carpet installer who had "very important customers." He proceeded to list the companies that he had as clients. My heart was saddened as I thought of this neglected child who deserved a small amount of time in his plans. But, remembering his eyeing-the-door, foot-tapping impatience at our first conference, I accepted his excuses, thinking a face-to-face conference would not yield any great results. "Well, since you are so busy, Mr. Day Planner, let's just call this a phone conference." (No, I didn't really call him that!)

In his widely-read book, *The Purpose-Driven Life*, Rick Warren writes, "Relationships take time and effort, and the best way to spell love is 'T-I-M-E.'" (p. 127,

Zondervan, 2002) It seems from my side of the desk that some children need more "love."

Required reading: *Be very careful, then, how you live, not as unwise, but as wise, making the most of every opportunity, because the days are evil. Ephesians 5:15,16*

Homework: If your school has an after-school program, walk past it about 5:45 to see which students are waiting for parents to pick them up. Give that child a little more of your attention this week. Perhaps you could eat lunch together or talk a little more during recess. The children who must stay on campus that long need a little more T-I-M-E.

Sense-ability

Preschool children are generally filled with self-confidence. Ask any group of kindergartners, "Can you sing? Dance? Do gymnastics? Skate? Play the piano?" The answers are "Yes, yes, yes, yes, and yes!" Five-year-old Megan was filling out a Sunday School booklet called "All About Me." The culminating statements were open-ended fill-in-the-blanks. After "Things I like about God," Megan wrote "Pawr," and following "Things I don't understand about God," she gave a definitive "nun." She knew everything about God when she was five. Theologians take notice. Go to kindergarten to get answers to the ponderous questions of life! Somewhere between the ages of five and ten children discover that they are not as proficient in all areas as they had once thought.

But I've decided that one of the reasons that they know so much when they are young is that they make full use of all five of their senses. When they are learning something they look, listen, sniff, taste, and touch. Maybe that's why teachers of young children refer to so many of them as "active learners." And the understanding teachers appreciate the busy noise and movement necessary to learn with your entire body.

We have a family joke about the "A" encyclopedia. When our children were young, families had no Internet to rely on. The main source of information was the set of encyclopedia that were in every school and most homes. To help young families get this wonderful set of books, Kroger Grocery Store had a promotion so you could buy one book each week. To help reel you in, the store offered the "A" book for only nine cents and subsequent volumes for $1.99. Unfortunately, the A encyclopedia was the only one we could afford. We jokingly told the children to raise their hands very quickly when the teacher gave assignments and volunteer to do reports on Alaska, aardvarks, Argentina, or anteaters. But even with the entire set of encyclopedia our children would, at best, learn only with two senses. Regrettably, it is easier to assign reports, which use only seeing and hearing, than to approach learning with the full range of sensation.

What Sunday School student wouldn't love to be in my friend Deanna's class? Her lesson on Jonah was given in a dark room with the scent of tuna fish from an open can and a spray bottle misting the children! Or maybe they would love to be in my friend Wilmojean's class. She taught the entire Seder or Passover meal around a large table with barbecue for the roasted lamb and parsley for the bitter herbs. Neither of these ladies was a degreed teacher, but they knew one very important thing about children: Teaching young children should never rely solely on seeing and hearing.

I think most young students are kinesthetic learners. This was shown in a delightful way on a recent trip with 100 first graders to the local IMAX Theatre. We went to see the movie, "Ocean Wonderland 3-D" as a culminating activity for an ocean unit. All over the theatre there were sounds of hands clapping together as they attempted to capture the water animals that seemed to be coming straight toward us. Failure did not deter this group as the reaching and clapping continued 40 minutes into the film.

Once a year, when I finish the planned units in social studies, I like to bring in my collection of Japanese souvenirs and toys. Now I have never set foot on the island, but we have had visitors from Japan in our home who have given us many things. At first, I wondered if I should let the children handle the items, or if I should hold them up for the class to see. I looked at the delicate fan, the tea set, the postcards, the silk scarves, and decided the very best use for them would involve first graders and touching. So, once a year, we touch, dress up, play with the toys, and experience Japan.

An activity that involves touching along with listening is even better. During our Five Senses unit, I fill eight glasses with varying levels of water and let the children play tunes with spoons. Since I use glasses that my husband got as a gasoline station promotion, instead of crystal, the pitch is not perfect, but the occasional loss of a glass is not catastrophic. We have a discussion before the music begins about the eventuality of breakage. I let them know that if it is an accident, it's all right.

Children also like to taste. I am saddened by the restrictions on food in public school classrooms. Multi-cultural studies are mandated by the state, then manacled, by banning food. What better way to experience Germany, France, Mexico, and the U.S. than with a taste of pretzels, pastries, nachos, and popcorn? Parents were glad to help with food donations for the tasting lessons. The teacher even learned a lesson from these classes. You don't ask a Vietnamese family to send refried beans. I got a nice can of pork and beans which I took home and traded for Mexican frijoles.

Young children move. They have not yet learned the adult deceptive practice of looking "toward" a speaker even if the topic does not interest them. Primary teachers need a dog-and-pony-show that changes every 10-15 minutes. The good news is this – most children like whatever dog and pony you present, if presented enthusiastically. Spelling, math, science – they are interested in every subject that is made palatable in presentation. What child can resist the bait of a teacher saying, "Today we are going to have so much fun that you will have to wipe the smiles off your faces?" I occasionally say this, and once I looked back to see Andrew intermittently wiping his smile off, smiling again, and wiping it off.

Recently I was thinking about when I feel most alive. I think it is when I am using all of my senses. The reason my family prefers going on a vacation instead of renting an inexpensive travelogue video is because we like to actually see the views, hear the music, taste the food, smell the countryside, and touch everything not guarded by security!

I received a forwarded letter called "The Seven Wonders of the World." A group of students were asked to list what they thought were the present greatest wonders of the world. The class came up with Egypt's Great Pyramid, the Taj Mahal, the Grand Canyon, the Panama Canal, the Empire State Building, St. Peter's Basilica, and the Great Wall of China.

While gathering votes the teacher noted that one student had not finished. The girl admitted that she was having a little trouble. "I couldn't quite make up my mind because there were so many." Then she read her list. "I think the Seven Wonders of the World are:

1. To see
2. To hear
3. To touch
4. To taste
5. To feel
6. To laugh, and
7. To love"

The children in our care are no different. They love to "experience." When, during the school day, do children have a chance to be most alive and use all of their senses? I have given this some thought and decided that it is at lunchtime. Why not bring the "alive" experience of lunch into the classroom as much as possible? Going beyond sight and hearing and also using the senses of taste, smell, and touch may pay big dividends for our young learners who first found out about the world by putting everything into their mouths!

Required reading: *But blessed are your* **eyes** *because they* **see***, and your* **ears** *because they* **hear***. For I tell you the truth, many prophets and righteous men longed to* **see** *what you see, but did not* **see** *it, and to* **hear** *what you* **hear** *but did not* **hear** *it. Matthew: 13:16,17*
The Lord **smelled** *the pleasing* **aroma**... *(of Noah's burnt offering) Genesis 8:21a*

Taste *and see that the Lord is good…Psalm 34:8a*
People were bringing little children to Jesus to have him **touch** *them, but the disciples rebuked them. And he took the children in his* **arms**, *put his* **hands** *on them and blessed them. Mark 10:13,16*

Homework: If you are in a school that can have food in the classroom, try the following: Eat split pea soup when you read *George and Martha* by James Marshall. Eat chicken soup with rice, of course, when you read, learn the months, and sing *Chicken Soup with Rice* by Maurice Sendak. Eat vegetable soup that you make in a crockpot after you read and, of course, act out *Stone Soup* by Marcia Brown or Ann McGovern.

Teachers Shouldn't Keep Sugar Ghosts in Their Closets

One of my delightful teaching buddies, Sarah, was new to first grade. She had read about an art project for Halloween that she wanted to try. She soaked yards of cheesecloth in sugar water and draped them over bottles and milk containers to form ethereal "ghosts" when dry. Her room became a veritable haunted house for Halloween. But, on November 1, Sarah couldn't bear to get rid of her cute creations. Nor could she on December 1, January 1, February 1…you get the picture. She stored the ghosts in her closet when she left for summer break. In August she returned to a roomful of cockroaches munching away on ghost meat! And, if you have even seen what Texans call "cockroaches," you will know that it took extensive extermination and death of ghosts to get the roach problem corrected.

Sweet Sarah was more than ready to give us her recipe for the project, but no one really wanted to give it a try. But often teachers have good ideas, terrific ones even, that are kept hidden in their closet. Creative lessons have sometimes been hidden "under a bushel" whether out of fear of seeming to be bragging or simply from not having enough time to share ideas with other teachers. Or sometimes there is a more sinister reason.

I taught kindergarten in a school in Indiana that reportedly lost a third grade teacher every year. It seems that two of the three third grades were being taught by best friends. The two shared only with each other and were in cahoots to get the best furniture, best books, and even the best students in their classes. The third teacher, the odd man out, spent her days with mismatched furniture, old books, difficult students, and then was ostracized at lunch and after school. I guess the principal did not catch on to the dynamics at that grade level, or he was too intimidated to say, "The jig is up!" No wonder there was a yearly turnover. Sharing was not taught at their universities, it seemed.

A close friend of mine had a different problem. She was extremely innovative and had been hired to teach in a district where there were many negative teachers. At lunch she would try to share some idea that had worked in her class only to get the discouraging platitude, "It won't work in my class." She finally transferred to a different district where teachers readily give and accept ideas.

I had the unique opportunity recently to swap teacher stories with one of my former first-graders, now a teacher in a nearby school. As we sat on the outdoor patio of Taco Cabana, enjoying an evening of visiting and good Mexican food, Holly asked if I had any good ideas for an upcoming unit.

"Do you have any great lesson plans for "Rocks?" she asked.

Remembering the Rock unit brought memories of boys and girls with flared nostrils and extreme excitement the past spring. "Oh, yes," I exclaimed. "I love to teach about rocks. Each child can gather a dozen rocks in an egg carton labeled "My Rock Collection," name them, weigh them, measure them…"

Holly's eyes glistened as the conversation became more animated.

"And then you do the scratch test with fingernails, copper pennies, and steel nails."

She was making mental notes.

"Try putting them in vinegar to see if acid will cause them to bubble and erode. Then drop them into a large bowl of water to see if they sink or float."

Holly had a great idea for an art extension of the science unit. We could paint rocks, add eyes, and make pet rocks and…"

Our voices rose as we added to this verbal unit on rocks. Suddenly we stopped, grew quiet, and looking around at others on the patio, burst into laughter. No doubt anyone overhearing this exchange would have been wondering if we had lives outside of the classroom. They probably wondered, "Who are these people who get so excited over rocks?"

Too bad Sarah couldn't have been with us that evening. She probably would have shared her recipe for sugar ghosts.

Required reading: *Command them to do good, to be rich in good deeds; and to be generous and willing to share. I Timothy 6:18*

Homework: Go to a new teacher or another colleague today and give them an idea for an activity that worked in your class.

November

Horse Sense

Eight-year-old Megan was in the back of the van clutching a thick volume ostensibly called *The United States Pony Club Manual of Horsemanship* by Susan E. Harris. Megan was supposed to have the first chapter read before her next riding lesson. Playing had been so much more interesting than reading the thick manual with the long words. So, in frenzy, she began reading quickly as her dad Scott drove her to the farm for the lesson.

Sensing her desperation, I, Grannie, decided to help her. I read page 11 as fast as I could. "Riding and caring for a pony can teach them [children] kindness, patience, responsibility, and perseverance, while taking instructions and working with other young riders can help instill self-discipline, good sportsmanship, and self-esteem."

"Wow," Megan interrupted, "it seems like horses can teach you the Fruit of the Spirit." The van erupted in laughter as we thought of horses extrapolating on *Galatians 5:22-23a*. *"But the fruit of the spirit is love, joy, peace, patience, kindness, goodness, faithfulness, gentleness and self-control."*

As Megan grew older and her family actually acquired some horses, we found out that not all horses are capable of teaching the Fruit of the Spirit. In fact, some are even the epitome of the "acts of the sinful nature!" Each of their three horses has a different temperament, not always under the Master's control. Rita, a Thoroughbred, often remains aloof and arrogant—untouchable. She lacks most of the good traits. Top Gun, a Morgan, is demanding and greedy. When he feels hunger pains, he neighs, stamps his hooves, and butts the barn door with his head. Patience, gentleness, and self-control are not in his personality. Only little Ellie, a miniature horse, has the attributes of a saint. She gladly suffers small children on her back, patiently waits for alfalfa, and then lets Top Gun eat first. She is loving, kind, patient, and gentle. She is a model horse, loved by the family and even by the two larger horses (except at mealtime!)

Megan has learned more from these horses than she did from the huge manual, and she has learned that God's truths are everywhere.

These nine virtues should be what every teacher desires. How do you get them? They aren't for sale, can't be learned in Fruit of the Spirit 101, or in a class on horsemanship. They are simply the outgrowth of the Spirit of the Lord in your life.

Required reading: *Live as children of the light (for the fruit of the light consists in all goodness, righteousness and truth) and find out what pleases the Lord. Ephesians 5:8b-10*

Homework: Take a sticky note and write one of the "fruits" on it that you want more of in your own life. Put it on your desk. Then tell the One who gives good gifts to His children what you need.

Nurse Slips

Our school has a very efficient health care system. The sending teacher fills out a no-carbon-required slip, sends the infirm or injured to the clinic where the child is tended to and returned to the classroom with a complete report on the same slip. The one downside is the interruption in the teaching time to fill out all of the lines on the form – date, time, sending teacher, homeroom teacher, and complaint. So much time could be saved by pre-writing the forms. Then only the child's name would need to be inserted. For example, the most common complaint could be written in - "Bumped head." The time would be - "Recess." Nurses brace for first grade recess time. Since teachers are required to send head bumps to the clinic, regardless of the severity, the natural clumsiness of first graders keeps nurses from eating lunch until late in the school day. One child even figured out the unwritten head-bumping rule and was seen thrashing his own head into playground equipment to get to go to the clinic.

Occasionally, there will be a different kind of complaint. Billy complained to his teacher that his toe hurt. "Which one?" my friend Janine asked kindly.

"The thumb toe," he said.

Billy probably got to go see the pretty nurses. I personally think that mean old nurses should be hired at elementary schools, but instead, beautiful women with the gentleness of angels are in charge of boo-boo's, homesickness, fevers, and even wet pants. Going to the clinic provides respite and relaxation in a child's busy day.

I always cringe when I receive verbal instructions early in the day from a concerned mother via the child. The message is usually "Mom says to send me to the nurse if I start feeling bad." I could begin filling out the nurse slip with everything but the time because that child **would** be going to the nurse. How I wish parents would write me a discreet note in **cursive** to give me a heads up on the child's health.

At times real injuries or illnesses need attention. The good news is that you flat cannot spook a primary teacher. We have seen head lice, dental caries, and fifth disease. We have seen blisters, fire ant stings, and throw-up.

Sometimes medical problems even make their way into classroom discussions. I was reviewing our study of the dictionary one morning. I asked if anyone remembered what we could learn from using a dictionary. Knowing that we can learn how to spell a word was easy. Knowing that we can also learn the meaning of a word was a little harder to verbalize. Finally Joel had it. He yelled out, "Like if you didn't know what 'constipated' means, you could look in the dictionary!"

I could not resist asking. "What does it mean?" I asked dumbly.

"Like when you eat too much cheese."

OK, look it up. Right there between "consternation" and "constituent," you will find it –

"kon'-ste-pat'-id – Having eaten too much cheese."

Occasionally children really will be sick and need to be sent home. When the child returns, an absence note from the parent is supposed to accompany him. Tracy did not have one, so she tore off a corner of yellow paper, drew a smiley face with something on its forehead and wrote the words "BIG FEVEr" in capital and lowercase letters. I generally get a clue that the notes are not from the parent when the child signs it "Mom" or misspells the mother's name!

James was one little guy who knew exactly where good health originates. One day I asked the class to write a story so good that I would "publish" it at my publishing company, "Put Your Name on Your Paper, Inc." (Otherwise known as my computer and printer at the back of the room.)

Taking the challenge seriously, James waxed eloquent: "God is a good man. He is a king. God died on the cross for you and me. God is good all the time. I love God. He is my savior, my **healer**, too." It went on for 87 more words of praise and testimony. It was "published" and read to the class. James was invited to come to my retirement party to give the prayer. Who would not want a little man of such conviction and faith in God's saving and healing power to pray you into retirement? I hear the nurse slips for the elderly are incrementally more difficult to fill out.

Required reading: *Jesus answered them, "It is not the healthy who need a doctor but the sick. I have not come to call the righteous, but the sinners to repentance." Luke 5:31, 32*

Homework: For Nurse Appreciation Week (or anytime) ask the children to write to the clinic staff, telling them how they have helped them in the past. Get ready for some laughter – the best medicine!

No Boundaries

Our school was blessed with a military family with two wonderful sons. Both boys had multiple sclerosis, a disease that destroys the sheaths that insulate nerve cells. This, in turn, causes weakness in the affected body part. The older son had weakness in his legs. The younger son Scott who was in my class had a weakness in his mouth. But, this sweet, positive family raised their boys to be winners – literally!

Every year our school has a talent show near the end of the year. No prizes or places are awarded, but everyone knew who won when Scott brought the house down with his rendition of the John Denver classic, "Country Roads." No disability could stop him.

I should not have been surprised when the bicycle rodeo winners were announced. Tears filled my eyes as the intercom came on to give the results. The brother with the paralysis in his legs won first place in the third grade competition.

I have thought about the brothers many times over the years. I don't know where they are now or what they are doing, but I bet they are still winners. They had learned to excel at the very point of their disability.

Required reading: *But he said to me, "My grace is sufficient for you, for my power is made perfect in weakness." Therefore I will boast all the more gladly about my weaknesses, so that Christ's power may rest on me. That is why, for Christ's sake, I delight in weaknesses, in insults, in hardships, in persecutions, in difficulties. For when I am weak, then I am strong. II Corinthians 12:9, 10*

Homework: What handicap or deficiency do you have? Use that very weakness this week. Do you have problems with organization? Stay late and clean out a file. Do you have problems with planning? Go ahead and get next week's plans all in order. Is there a subject that you dislike teaching? Ask someone for help in planning a terrific lesson in that area.

Kiddie Lit

Bookstores are a haven in the mall. Elementary teachers are drawn instinctively to the children's section. When new book orders are distributed in class, teachers pore over the selections as happily as the students. Let's face it – teachers love children's literature! At my home I have a bookcase of very worn paperback books that have been loved by me and many classrooms full of children over the years. Even some of my favorite quotable lines are from children's literature. Dr. Seuss' *Did You Ever Think How Lucky You Are?* has a line that only teachers really understand:

> "And how fortunate you're not Professor DeBreeze
> Who has spent the past 32 years, if you please,
> Trying to teach Irish ducks to read Jivenese."

Oh, yes, we can really identify! There were days when I thought my "Irish ducks" would never learn to read "Jivenese."

Children learn very early to treasure their favorite books. One day Jenny brought me a very loved copy of H. A. Rey's *Curious George* that needed major triage. I told her, as is my custom, to put it on my desk in the red basket. (Every teacher needs a red basket for all sorts of collections!) She eyed me warily. "What are you going to do with it?"

I hemmed and hawed about how old and crispy the pages had become. She saw through the verbiage and asked worriedly, "Is it going to Book Heaven?"

Another day in a class discussion on reading at home, I was extolling the virtues and enjoyment of books. "Don't you love to read in bed?" I asked. "Every night Before I go to sleep I read the Bible."

Don looked at me, mentally calculated how many years this might have been going on, and asked, "Haven't you finished it yet?"

Justin, a bright and very active learner, had been in The Word himself, trying to memorize the books of the Old Testament in order. His friend Zachery did not appreciate Justin's studies as he came to me and complained, "Justin keeps calling me 'Deuteronomy.'"

When our daughter Julie was young, we decided to read all of the Newbery Medal Books together, a lofty goal. Needless to say, we did not make it. But, in the process, we enjoyed many wonderful stories. Reading together gave us common ground, common friends, and common experiences. *Miracles on Maple Hill* warmed our hearts, *Sounder* made us cry, but gave us a memorable quote: "There's no story as good as the story of Joseph!"* Our book friends were so much a part of our family that I sent the adult Julie a picture of me standing by the fountain near the Metropolitan Museum of Art in New York City. But I knew that she would really rather have had a picture of me "in" the fountain like the children in the Newbery prize winning book, *From the Mixed-Up Files of Mrs. Basil E. Frankweiler* . **

Books, even children's books, can have a profound influence on a child's thinking about monumental topics like life and death. In the spring I got a note from Mercedes that might have seemed strange if I did not remember a wonderful story that we had shared together. She wrote, [sic] "Wen you die I will put or pour you'r favorite thing to eat on you'r cofen." I knew that this was a great tribute since the children in *Chicken Sunday* by Patricia Polacco pour chicken broth all over the grave of a beloved grandmother. Because we had enjoyed this delightful story, I did not find her note macabre, but magnanimous. This child heard a story and actually made friends with the characters, letting their story go into her heart and give voice to her own love.

The written word – how powerful! No wonder God chose to call His own Son "The Word."

Required reading: *In the beginning was the word, and the word was with God, and the word was God. He was with God in the beginning. John 1:1, 2*

Homework: Check out a copy of *Chicken Sunday* by Patricia Polacco, and let your class enjoy the "slow thunder and sweet rain" of this loving story based on an event in Ms. Polacco's life.

*Sounder by William H. Armstrong, p. 102

**From the Mixed Up Files of Mrs. Basil E. Frankweiler by E. L. Konigsburg

December

Stealing Home

Walking in our neighborhood is especially delightful in December. I can see which neighbors have begun Christmas decorating and which ones have just plugged in the lights they left on their house all year long. Walking along one morning by myself, I caught this exchange between a very young child and her grandmother concerning a yard decoration that was missing.

"They took Frosty, Gramma?"

"Yes, some bad people took Frosty."

"They took Frosty, Gramma?"

"Yes, they took Frosty, and there's only one thing we can hope."

"What, Gramma?"

I slowed my pace and strained to hear Gramma's words to her grandchild. Perhaps she would give the child hope of Frosty's return, of repentance of the bad guys, or perhaps of being able to get a new Frosty.

"We can hope that something really bad happens to them."

Well, there ya have it. A veritable Old Testament grandma – eye for an eye retribution. Her answer left me wishing for a better explanation for an impressionable child.

Sometimes the adult/child interchange has a different twist with the child having the right answer. My friend

Denise was at a Wednesday night church service with her five-year-old daughter Jenna when she got the news that thieves were breaking into her home, making off with their belongings, even rolling out a giant refrigerator toward their truck. The police had been called, and Denise felt she should return home as soon as possible. Getting Jenna from her class and into the car, Denise drove as fast as possible down McAllister Freeway toward their home. Denise's thoughts were interrupted by Jenna's tiny voice in the back seat. "Mommy, should we pray?"

"Yes, Jenna," Denise said. "You pray. Mommy's driving." Denise, worrying about the amount of the loss, hoping that the police had interrupted their malfeasance before too much was taken, was shocked by the sweet prayer coming from the back seat.

"Dear Jesus, some bad guys have been in our house, taking our stuff. They probably don't know you. We just pray that they will get Jesus in their hearts and not do these bad things. Amen."

Denise felt shame that her thought had been on worldly goods when Jenna was concerned with the eternal salvation of the thieves. Perhaps Jenna needs to visit the little girl who had lost her Christmas snowman – and with her gramma, too.

Required reading: *Do not take revenge, my friends, but leave room for God's wrath, for it is written: "It is mine to avenge; I will repay, says the Lord." Roman 12:19*

Homework: Have you ever had anything stolen in your classroom? Remember to pray for the thief, even as you track down the culprit.

Peace, Joy, Brags, and Lies

Christmas was over. We had come through the pre-Christmas excitement very well.

I always choose Mexico as my country to teach to all five first grades during the December multi-cultural unit. Since I love theater arts, we act out the Legend of the Poinsettia and Las Posadas, complete with unlit candles and costumes. We look at Mexican souvenirs, listen to the story of the Mexican flag and the Christmas story, learn some geography, speak some Spanish, dance to Mariachi music, and eat candy after pretending to break a piñata. Extreme energy is required to teach this five times. I jokingly told a friend that, by the fifth class, I want to say, "They don't have Christmas in Mexico, boys and girls. Just color your picture."

After the Christmas break, the children returned with stories of trips and toys. Then on January 6, Eric, a precious and happy child, came to school telling about toys he had received on that day, Día de Los Reyes. Three Kings Day is widely celebrated in Mexico on January 6, the twelfth day of Christmas.

"Eric," I whined in mock disbelief, "I remember that you got gifts on Christmas Day, and now… more gifts? I don't get two Christmases. What is the deal here?"

"Well," he said smiling, "if you were a Mexican like me, you would!"

Christmas… a time of peace, joy… brags… and lies…

Our tiny firstborn granddaughter Megan was only 23 months old at Christmas time. She was asked what she wanted as gifts. She answered sweetly, "Necklace, fruit snacks, candy, bubbles." She got all of these modest gifts and much more that year.

She did have one fault that Christmas, however. Her mom Julie had two nativity sets with Mary, Joseph, and Baby Jesus - one made of glass and the other made of plastic. Megan would constantly get the glass Baby Jesus, climb onto her tiny step stool, and bathe him in the bathroom sink. Julie tried in vain to explain to Megan that it would be OK to wash the plastic baby, but not the breakable one. Megan later explained that she had heard adults say that we should "wash up" (worship) Jesus, so she was just following that suggestion.

One day as Julie went out to the garage to get meat from the freezer, she heard water running in the bathroom. Rushing in, Julie caught Megan wet-handed, getting ready to give the breakable baby his morning bath.

"Megan!" scolded Julie.

Megan looked innocent, explaining, "He falled in the water!"

Christmas, a time of peace, joy, brags, and lies.

Required reading: *While they were there, the time came for the baby to be born, and she gave birth to her firstborn, a son. She wrapped him in cloths and placed him in a manger, because there was no room for them in the inn. Luke 2:6, 7*

Homework: Save all of your old Christmas cards and cut off the fronts. Next year you'll have a ready supply of pictures to glue onto construction paper cards. Let the children write messages of hope and love inside and deliver them to the nearest nursing home.

'Riting Around the Christmas Tree

One of my favorite Christmas activities is to ask the children to write the words to the Christmas song that they love most. The results are precious. Here is our first grade songbook. I'm sure you will recognize them. [sic]

The Frst Nolil

The frst nolil the aejele did sa
Was to shrpin for sheprs in fiels as thae lae.
In fiels war keeping thar shep
No a coed witrs nilht thar was so dep
Nolil, nolil,
Nolil, nolil

Rotof the Red Noese Roder
(Decorated with eighth and half
notes at the top of the page.)

Rotof the red noese ronder
Had a ver sin noese
If u eivre saw it
U eire sa it gose.

Alternate Version of Rouf the Red Noz Radnder

Rouf the red noz radn der
Had a shony noz
And if yuw avr sol him yuw wd evn thc it gloz.

But, my personal favorite is …

Hlalyo hlalyo
Hlalyo hlalyo
Hlalyo hlalyo
Hlalyo hlalyo
Puzzled? It's the "Hallelujah" Chorus, of course!
Primary teachers will applaud such noble writing attempts
only four months into first grade.

Required reading: *The kingdom of the world has become the kingdom of our Lord and of his Christ, and he will reign forever and ever. Revelation 11:15b*

Homework: Get a recording of the "Hallelujah" chorus and tell the story of how King George II stood when this last song of "The Messiah" was performed. Then tell the class that all day long you will try to trick them by playing the song while they are seated to see who will remember to stand like the king. They love this and will ask to play it again long after Christmas. And, I bet, even as adults, they will not forget to stand when it is played.

Poor

"Poor" is such a relative term. What we in the U.S. consider to be poverty might be a comfortable life in many third world countries. Children are touched by pictures or stories of poverty, even if they are in the throes of destitution themselves. Poor children often generously bring their own government rations for food bank drives and donate their own jar of pennies in a Make-a-Wish collection. Children, even poor ones, sometimes assume that everyone has money. In our class, Stephanie was poring over a small reader that showed different types of homes around the world. Some were very shoddy by American standards. Stephanie studied the pictures and asked, "How did they get so poor? Did they waste their money?"

It's not always easy for a teacher to know which children in a classroom are really poor. You get clues during the year. Poor children bring field trip money late and in small change as if couch cushions have been raided to come up with the fee. Poor children often return once-in-a-lifetime "missing teeth" pictures for lack of funds. Poor children are late many times because the car won't start.

Poverty is often a generational cycle. It takes a strong family to decide to break out. Teachers generally have compassion on poor children, but not always on their parents, particularly the parents who break the unwritten rules:

1. Teachers don't like smoking.
2. Teachers don't like dirt.
3. Teachers don't like neglect.

"Poor" parents who smoke get unsympathetic reviews from teachers. All health, religious, and social reasons aside, teachers hate the fact that smoking is expensive, very expensive. This habit takes money needed for school supplies, clothes, field trips, Tide, and vegetables. How do teachers know which parents smoke? They open the coat closet. Smoking parents who don't read the warnings on the pack of cigarettes also do not read the washing instructions on coats.

"Poor" does not have to mean dirty. One precious girl who was told to write a sentence using the word "good," wrote, "I go to the Goodwill." What a good sentence and a good place to get inexpensive clothing. I've shopped there myself. Hand-me-downs or second-hand clothes can be laundered. And bodies are washable.

"Poor" does not have to mean neglected. One year I had a sweet child whose mother was using drugs and neglecting her children. She generally looked pretty good herself, but Ross was unkempt and had long, dirty fingernails. I decided to give him some fingernail clippers in the time-honored teacher way – by rigging a Bingo game. I sauntered by Ross's desk several times during the game, eyeing which numbers he needed and later called them. Amazingly, Ross won! I handed him the clippers. He was thrilled to win this simple machine. He asked me, "What they do?" (Did I fail to mention that he also had syntax problems?) I explained the function to him, introducing him to the wonders of shorter nails.

There is a big difference between temporary and permanent poverty. The difference is hope. Permanent poverty seems to have no end – poverty extending into the future. It becomes a way of life. Temporary poverty would describe some college students and first time parents.

I remember well the days of decorating our house in what we jokingly called "early matrimony" style, complete with the compulsory brick and board bookcase so fashionable among the college couples. We also practiced "planned poverty" when we decided to have a child while still in college. We cannot eat tuna casserole to this day without thinking of those days. But we knew that, after college, we could hope to have a little more change in our pockets, so we endured the dearth for several years. I grew from this experience. I learned to sew, make drapes, and fix hamburger meat in enough different ways to fill a cookbook. Recycling was not a trendy activity but a necessity. I also learned what it means to budget and how carefully money has to be spent. I learned what Clifford Odets meant when he wrote "Life shouldn't be printed on dollar bills." I learned empathy for those whose poverty is not temporary.

Teachers have a responsibility to the poor children in their classes. We are responsible to not emphasize their condition or put undue pressure on them to purchase "extras" that cost money such as pictures, book clubs, book fairs, T-shirts, and Christmas bazaars. Teachers can couch requests for non-essential money items with a disclaimer. "If your parents say, 'No, we don't have the money,' that's OK."

Teachers can direct parents on a stringent budget to resources that they can use so their children are not the losers. Sometimes schools hire a parent liaison who is available to offer information on free health and dental clinics, low-cost clothes and glasses, or even job information. What some parents don't know is that even some wonderful youth sports organizations like the YMCA offer free or reduced-cost sports to low-income families.

Teachers can stress priorities in spending in units such as economics and money. Children easily understand the relative importance of goods and services.

Teachers can show good examples of determination and drive. Motivation is modeled! Our class was privileged to have a high school mentor named Jay. He was a humble young man who would always come into the classroom wearing his letter jacket with soccer awards on it. He became our class hero. The children adored him. I would quiz Jay in front of the children on his plans for the future, which included college and an engineering degree. Role models can inspire children to one day break the poverty cycle.

Teachers can remember their own poverty. One afternoon a group of four ladies from my church gathered at my house to practice music. During a break we got on the subject of being poor. Three of us were laughing, trying to outdo each with our tales of poverty. One lady did not talk, but listened curiously. Later she said, "I guess we never knew poverty. We have always had enough money." The group grew quiet – each of us feeling sorry for our friend who could not relate other as in trying to outdo each other with our tales of poverty.

Children must wonder if their well-clothed teachers have ever been poor. One upper elementary child commented, "People always say teachers don't get enough money, but I've seen their cars in the parking lot!"

Jesus left the riches of His Father to become poor in order to reach the world. Teachers who own fancy cars in the parking lot may have to learn to "think poor" in order to understand the dynamics of poverty.

Required reading: *For you know the grace of our Lord Jesus Christ, that though he was rich, yet for your sakes he became poor, so that you through his poverty might become rich. II Corinthians 8:9*

Homework: Set up a home reading program, sending home a book with a child every time he returns one with a signed slip stating that the book has been read. This way even the poorest in your class has access to appropriate reading material. Then give new books as monthly prizes for the most books read. This takes time, effort, and bookkeeping, but the results are phenomenal!

January

Get Out of Jail Free

January always brings stories of Ruby Bridges, Rosa Parks, and Dr. Martin Luther King, Jr. One day, long after our social studies lesson had ended, Ikey raised his hand. "Did they give her money back?" he asked earnestly.

"I'm sorry. What?" I answered dumbly.

"Rosa Parks. Did they give her money back?"

"I don't know," I answered honestly, trying to see where his questioning was leading.

"Well, they made her get off the bus. They should have given her money back. Then she would have some money to use to get out of jail when she was arrested."

I sat marveling at a question that begs to be answered. I wonder just who would know. But just as curious is the fact that a six year old child has knowledge of bail bonds.

Unfortunately, many children come into first grade having already seen the darker side of life. One such child was Kerry. I called her to my desk after a writing assignment. "Kerry," I said, holding her journal entry, "it looks like this says, 'Mother ran over daddy.'"

"It does," she answered openly. "My mom really did run over my dad. She had to go to jail. My grandma cried. My dad's family came over to beat her up, but she kept the door locked."

Sometimes a little knowledge of the justice system is a dangerous thing. Andre', writing a complimentary essay about his friend Eric, predicted, "You won't have to go to boob camp." I called Andre' to me to ask what he was trying to say. "You know, that place where bad kids go – boob camp."

"Oh, you meant to say 'boot camp' with a 't'," I corrected.

Bail bonds, assault, retribution – not exactly first grade subjects, but ones that occupy the minds of many of our young children. It was not uncommon to hear small children refer to juvenile detention with the familiar sounding term "juvie." A little girl in my class reports that her pregnant mother was thrown into a wall by her dad. A boy has to miss school to go to court for custody hearings.

Meanwhile, the teacher keeps teaching at the front of the room, trying to keep the attention of children whose minds are occupied with boot camp, arrests, custody, and jail.

School has to become an oasis in the dry, dry land where some of children live. School has to be a place of justice tempered with kindness.

Required reading: *Everyone must submit himself to the governing authorities, for there is no authority except that which God has established. For rulers hold no terror for those who do right, but for those who do wrong. Romans 13:1, 3*

Homework: Pray for the children in your class whose families are in the throes of legal problems, custody battles, drug problems, or divorce. Continue to expect good behavior from all children, knowing that those who learn obedience at home and school will have an easier time obeying civil authority and the ultimate authority of God.

Royal Rules

What little girl doesn't like royalty? I know I did. I can remember listening to the radio in 1953 as Elizabeth came Queen Elizabeth II. And, as an adult, I and millions of others were enamored with the lovely Diana wedding her Prince Charles. Royalty is impressive!

The closest we can come to American royals would probably be well-known people of politics, movies, sports, and TV. I was doing a little name-dropping in my class, hoping to impress them with a famous person I had actually seen. "I was at the graduation of my son-in-law at Anderson University. I got to hear a speech by the wife of Dr. Martin Luther King, Jr." The class was listening attentively since we had just studied his life story in social studies. "Her name is Coretta Scott King."

One little girl eyed me warily, thinking that I was gender confused. "Don't you mean Coretta Scott <u>Queen</u>?" she asked.

Actually, I have learned much about royalty over the years, and I have found out that I am a royal myself. My Father is a king. Miriam, one of the sweet girls in our Sunday School class, has a T-shirt that says, "I am a Princess. My Father is the King of Kings." I have always appreciated the fact that my "dad" owns it all, so it is all mine. I remember a song that I used to sing in my childhood that taught me this principle.

He owns the cattle on a thousand hills,
The wealth in every mine;
He owns the rivers and the rocks and rills,
The sun and stars that shine.
Wonderful riches, more than tongue can tell -
He is my Father, so they're mine as well;
He owns the cattle on a thousand hills -
I know that He will care for me.*

I sang this childhood song to myself on a bus tour of the Alps in Switzerland. I appreciated the beauty so much more, thinking that it all was mine!

Knowing that I am a princess gives me good self-esteem. Recently I was asked to speak in front of a large group of teachers, a fearsome task. I kept thinking about Miriam's T-shirt and reminding myself that "I am a Princess." It really helped.

Houston pastor Joel Osteen writes in *Your Best Life Now Journal*, "All my life, I've been aware of God's favor." He cites his mother's daily prayers including her petition to God that "Your hand of favor will always be upon them." (p. 23) He says this early confirmation of his position as a child of God has blessed his life. He expects, in a humble way, to be treated deferentially. How awesome is our vantage point to help children and fellow teachers to see, not the arrogance of this favor, but the confidence we possess in knowing who our "Dad" is!

Required reading: *The Spirit himself testifies with our spirit that we are God's heirs – heirs of God and co-heirs with Christ…Romans 8:17b*

Homework: What is the hardest thing you have to do today? It will help to remember that you are a Prince or a Princess if you have accepted the offer of the King of Kings to be His kid!

*"He Owns the Cattle on a Thousand Hills" Words and Music by John W. Peterson

Crystal Clear Clergy

We used to put phonics worksheets in the listening center. I'm sure many a first grade child had trouble in those days with my rule: No one is allowed to say "bored." I frightened one good parent when her son Chad came home from school and asked, "What is that 'b' word that Mrs. James won't let us say?" Suffice it to say that my listening center was extremely "dull."

One ordinary day the children were at the listening center, mindlessly marking the phonics worksheet and at least <u>thinking</u> the "b" word, when a miracle happened! A voice broke through on the tape player – not the monotone voice saying, "Mark the pictures that start with the same sound as '**ch**icken,'" but a voice preaching the gospel! What a welcome respite for the children at the insipid center.

One child, evidently from a different religious persuasion from this mysterious speaker, called out, "Mrs. James, there's a priest on here!" I, wanting to witness the supernatural on a pretty natural day, put the headset to my ear. Sure enough, a preacher was coming into his third point in an amplified voice.

How this happened I still don't know. Perhaps the electric wires over our portable had somehow been the conduit for a radio sermon. I don't understand radio waves or electricity, so I was not inclined to try to figure it out. I did, however, report the phenomenon to the office. "Look," I said, "there is a radio preacher being picked up by my tape player. I really don't mind it continuing if I can see some results." But changes in behavior did not come.

Another member of the clergy came to school, but this time as a welcomed guest. During our unit on community helpers I sent a note to invite any parent who wanted to come to social studies class to explain how they help people with their occupation. Over the years I have had visits from civilian and military firefighters, a pilot, a bank officer, an insulation installer, a surveyor, a small engine mechanic, a train engineer, and others. This year I received a note back from Rev. Fred Morgan, the local Presbyterian pastor. I gladly set up a time for a visit. I knew the Morgan family from having David, their older child, in my class. I knew Becca would be thrilled to "show off" her daddy. I also knew that Rev. Morgan would relate well to first graders.

Most community helpers bring the tools of their trade, and Rev. Morgan was no exception. He dressed in his clerical robe, collar and stole. He entered the classroom as an imposing figure, impressing the first graders with his height and the authority in his voice. He showed his Sunday wardrobe and then began to explain his duties.

"My job is to help people celebrate. Every Sunday people come to church to celebrate!" he said excitedly.

A little voice interrupted, "Could you come over to my house? My family loves to celebrate!"

The response was not one that either one of us had expected. We chuckled to ourselves that this child no doubt had visions of this nice man coming to his family's barbecue and laughing and joking with his aunts, uncles, and cousins on Sundays…

…but then, come to think of it, that's just the way Jesus ministered. He met people at their barbecues and taught them there.

Required reading: *When Jesus reached the spot, he looked up and said to him, "Zacchaeus, come down immediately. I must stay at your house today. So he came down at once and welcomed him gladly. All the people saw this and began to mutter, "He has gone to be the guest of a 'sinner.'" Luke 19:5-7*

Homework: Go to the next "celebration" that you are invited to – ball game, birthday party, or baptism. Be Jesus in tennis shoes!

The Comfort of
the Holy Spirit

It was Saturday before I even looked at the Sunday School lesson topic for the next day. "The Comfort of the Holy Spirit." The words leaped out from the teacher's manual, and my eyes widened. The thought of translating that important tenet from the Word of God to a classroom of 2nd through 5th graders added more stress to my life. Although I was a veteran Sunday School teacher with many years of public school experience, this seemed like an arduous task.

I sat down at the kitchen table and sighed. I knew from many years in Sunday School myself that comforting was one of the works of the Spirit of God. However, my life at present left little time for receiving comfort, only for giving. I tried to put aside the worries about my mother who was in the mid-stages of Alzheimer's disease, issues with my dad who had dementia, and the never-ending needs of the first graders in my classroom. I reminded myself that Jesus himself had promised that He would not leave us comfortless.

"The Comfort of the Holy Spirit..." I stared again at the black words on the white paper, then scanned the lesson looking for clues to help me bring this theology to our little group of South Texas children. One idea was to introduce the lesson by bringing in symbols of comfort to a child – a teddy bear, perhaps, or a blanket. I jumped up and scoured our empty-nest house, almost bereft of childhood symbols. I found a favorite and well-worn blanket and a Mickey Mouse stuffed toy. I also found a soft blue blanket that had been in my parents' home in happier days. I studied the scripture references and somehow put the lesson into a semblance of order. I was as ready as I could be at this time.

Sunday morning my husband and I arrived early at church and climbed the stairs to the cheerful classroom that would soon be filled with lively juniors.

We began the lesson by looking at the objects of comfort. They enjoyed seeing them and realizing that it is a common experience to need comfort. Then we spoke of fears that might need to be relieved through comfort. We brainstormed ideas of things that are scary to children – mean dogs, bad guys, getting hurt, losing your parents, state-mandated tests. It's easy to brainstorm when you are seven to eleven years old. And when you are seven to eleven years old, treacherous things are everywhere.

After each expressed fear, Jerry would wrap the snuggly blue blankets around that child's shoulders and say, "This is the comfort of the Holy Spirit." After each had a turn to be wrapped in the blue blanket, the children yelled, "Now, you go!"

I looked at our little class and told them quite honestly, "My mother has Alzheimer's and can't remember things. My fear is that I will lose my mind, too." Jerry approached me with the blue blanket, saying, "This is the comfort of the Holy Spirit."

There was a pause. Then Brody, one of our students, spoke up. "Can we come up and hug you?"

"Sure," I said. I was immediately engulfed in the loving arms of children, wrapping me in the comfort of the Holy Spirit. The teacher became the one taught.

The term now has a new and personal read for me. The comfort that is provided by the Holy Spirit can come to a person without human intervention just as the old hymn reminds us. "In His arms He'll take and shield thee – Thou wilt find a solace there."* But sometimes we need to see that comfort fleshed out as I did that Sunday morning in the love of little children.

Required reading: *Praise be to the God and Father of our Lord Jesus Christ, the Father of compassion and the God of all comfort, who comforts us in all our troubles, so that we can comfort those in any trouble with the comfort we ourselves have received from God. II Corinthians 1:3, 4*

Homework: Become that comfort for someone today – a child, a colleague, or a family member. And don't forget to accept encouragement that others offer to you.

*"What a Friend We Have in Jesus" by Joseph M. Scriven

February

Don't Put Words
in My Mouth

It was early February and still a bit cool in the mornings. Normally children who arrive in the room early are asked to report to the cafeteria. But on this particular day, Justin stuck his head into the room only a minute or two before the bell was scheduled to ring. I told him that I would not send him to the cafeteria since it was almost time for the children to be dismissed to come to the classrooms. He came in very happily since it is very important to be first in the room. Or first in line. Or first anywhere. That's why they are called "first" graders! When the rest of the class entered the room, Justin reported the reason for his being first in the room. "Mrs. James said, 'What the heck, come on in…it's your birthday!'" Now that was putting words in my mouth!

It's one thing to put words in your teacher's mouth, but yet another to speak for the Almighty. Our son Rick who had just turned three loved to listen to the news. In 1974 much of the news had to do with conservation of energy. American had been experiencing a shortage of gasoline and electricity. One night he pulled his tiny rocker close to the TV set since he heard that President Gerald Ford was going to be speaking that evening. At the end of this televised speech, President Ford made a plea for reduction in use of gas and electric power. He pled in words that even our baby could understand. "When you aren't using them, turn off the lights…" and again he encouraged, "…we are not going to be afraid of the dark, any of us."

Later that night as I was tucking Rick into bed, I jokingly told him that we would be turning out his night light from now on at the President's request. I could see a look of consternation as he surveyed his limited three-year-old mental file to see who could trump the President. Finally, he had it! He slowly tried out his rebuttal on me. "But, God came down from the sky and said, 'Turn your lights on, everybody!'"

You can bet that Rick's night light stayed on that night and for as long as he needed it, national crisis notwithstanding.

Required reading: *Jesus answered, "It is written, 'Man does not live on bread alone, but on every word that comes from the mouth of God.'" Matthew 4:4*

Homework: Be on the lookout for verbally creative children who may not get the words or spelling quite right, but who have a message. Challenge them this week to use that creativity without bounds. Don't even expect all of the facts to be correct. Clean up their spelling by typing it yourself on the computer and putting it in book form. Let them see that you appreciate their creative thinking. Let the child illustrate the book and read it to the class, the principal, his parents, or other classes.

Star Quality

Our daughter Julie loves playing board games, so it was inevitable that she would teach her daughters to enjoy all kinds of non-electronic games. Julie found the old game "Careers," called her eight-year-old daughter Megan to play with her, and the two highly competitive girls began the game.

At one point Julie read a statement for Megan to answer. "Name your favorite star."

Megan thought very hard, and then answered, "Orion's Belt, I guess." Julie suppressed a giggle, then explained that this was probably referring to movie stars, rock stars, or sports stars, instead of planetary stars.

Visibly struggling, Megan finally came up with the name of an NBA star, then with the Sacramento Kings. "I don't have any star that I like, but I want to win, so I guess I'll say 'Jason Williams' just so that I can get the points. But I really think that he is kind of dumb. I'd rather stick with 'Orion's Belt.'"

I have never taught a student who became a true star, as in "household word." But I have had many who have had their 15 minutes of fame, at least in the teachers' lounge. One such student was my adorable Sarita. Blessed with very long and curly hair and a free spirit, Sarita gave me many laughs and stories to share.

This brunette Shirley Temple was on the playground after lunch on a warm day when she suddenly and dramatically ripped off her jumper. My student teacher gasped, "Sarita, you can't do that!"

"It's OK," she reasoned, "I have a shirt and shorts on underneath."

"But, look," Ms. Mesa tried to reason, "our school rules say that your shorts have to be as long as your fingertips when you put your hands by your sides."

Sarita measured with her hands and realized that the difference in shorts length and fingertips was huge. "Oh," she bemoaned, "my arms are too long!"

The student teacher and I had a good laugh privately over her misplaced blame. Her phrase has also become a family joke. I told my husband about Sarita's perceived anatomical problems. Later that week, we were being shown to our table in one of our favorite Mexican restaurants. Our hostess was a tall thin girl with very short shorts. I punched Jerry and mouthed, "Her arms are too long!"

Sarita's innocence was in sharp contrast to other children who are exposed to rock stars, adult movies, and inappropriate literature at such an early age that they seem to have never experienced childhood at all. One such child was Sandy. Her stated career choice in first grade was "rock star." One day she was singing a song she had heard on the radio. James, sitting near her, had his senses and sensitivity offended. He ran to me and complained all in one breath, "Mrs. James, please tell Sandy to stop singing that song, because I'm saved, and I'm not supposed to listen to that kind of music!"

Not having time at that moment to lecture the worldly musician, I reprimanded her quickly and turned my attention to James. "Sweetie, I'm saved, too, but Jesus says we are 'in the world, but not of it.' Sometimes we just have to ignore things like this."

James gave me a very blank look at my "in, but not of" speech, but it was the best I could come up with in the middle of social studies. Somehow, I know he will learn this lesson later over and over and over.

Required reading: *He determines the number of the stars and calls them each by name." Psalm 147:4*

Homework: Introduce your children to stars who shine with good works. Hold up role models that are to be emulated. The world of music, movies, and sports has such stars – point them out by reading about their good deeds from the newspapers, books, or the Internet. San Antonio has been blessed with a great role model for children in David Robinson, retired Spurs player.

It's the Law

The story of Abraham Lincoln is such a powerful one, full of triumphs and tragedies and the total Americana of being "born in a log cabin." I love to teach lessons on Lincoln. The children and I both enjoy the book, *True Stories About Abraham Lincoln*, by Ruth Belov Gross because of the short vignettes told in first grade language. As we read this book over several days, we also do Lincoln projects.

The children roll tiny brown paper logs on pencils, slide them off and glue them onto clean milk cartons to make tiny log cabins. The cabins are then put into villages on large green butcher paper, and the fun begins. Small plastic animals are doled out and a variety of materials are available to use – craft sticks, tissue paper, clay, seeds, artificial flowers, and metal foil. The children "fence" their property and make foil ponds and "plant" seed gardens. Creativity runs high as small pebbles, gathered at recess, are glued down paths or around ponds. Historical timelines can be discussed as children talk about making cars or TV antennas. The villages get more and more elaborate as days go by. I begin to get a mental image of the proverbial bell shape curve with perfection of this project coming at the peak of the curve. This occurs on about day two. Any further work after that and the project's faultlessness begins to slide down the right side into excess.

We make paper towel rolls into Lincoln puppets and reenact chapters from the *True Stories About Abraham Lincoln* book. They rock tiny Abe, argue court cases as the adult Abraham, and get sworn in as President Lincoln.

One year I had a particularly creative class who transformed a huge refrigerator box into a log cabin using leftover wrapping paper rolls from the local "Elf Louise" Christmas center and many, many hot glue sticks. They decorated the inside with scenes from the life of Lincoln and gave tours of the cabin in the front hall.

One of the chapters about Lincoln has to do with his becoming a self-taught lawyer. To understand this, the children needed to know what a lawyer does. I explained that a lawyer talks for you if you are in trouble. "For example," I said, grasping for a pertinent illustration, "what if a man said that I killed his dog, and I didn't do it. I would hire a lawyer to help me tell the judge that I was innocent."

Justin, indignant at such an accusation, even a pretend one, against his teacher, came to my defense. "How could you?" he demanded. "You work all week. You stay home Saturday, and you go to church on Sunday! You couldn't do it!" I haven't seen Justin for several years, but I hope his plans include law school. He would make a great defense attorney.

In 1995 I didn't have to explain about lawyers in too much detail. Every home, it seems, was addicted to a televised trial which parents watched daily. One day that year I complained that it was the 100th anniversary of the first printing of the song "America the Beautiful" by Katherine Lee Bates, and I hadn't heard anything about that on TV. One bright little girl spoke up, "Well, if they would get that O. J. trial off TV, you might!"

To review the life of Lincoln, I was posing open-ended statements to check for understanding. "Lincoln was a lawyer. You get a lawyer if you are…"

"Rich!" exclaimed Emmanuel. He must have been following the O.J. trial very carefully!

Required reading: *Why don't you judge for yourself what is right? As you are going with your adversary to the magistrate, try hard to be reconciled to him on the way, or he may drag you off to the judge, and the judge turn you over to the officer, and the officer throw you into prison. Luke 12:57-58*

Homework: Community helpers can be taught all year long as you study the lives of famous Americans. Try getting an anthology of well-known people and reading a chapter now and then to broaden career choices beyond teacher, fireman, policeman, and ballerina.

The Walls Came Tumblin'!

Old Testament stoires are more than just history lessons. They contain many life lessons as well. My husband and I had been teaching about Moses, the 40-year desert marathon, spies into the land of Canaan – the sequential stories about man's faithlessness and God's faithfulness—to our Sunday class of Juniors for several weeks. Finally, the lesson was about the walls of Jericho tumblin' down!

We knew that our class of seven to eleven year olds would love to do more than **hear** the story; they would love to **be** the story! We set up makeshift "walls" out of books that we had in the classroom. We planned our attack of the walls. We would circle the walls once a day for the first six days. Then, on the seventh day, we would travel seven times around the city. The adult class next door not only tolerated our lively bunch, but actually celebrated them. Even so, this Sunday's play-acting would certainly be fodder for guessing about the lesson when the trampling of feet began.

It was fun to circle the room thirteen times, imagining ourselves getting ready to take the city. Around and around the books we marched until the signal was given on the ram's horn, and we all gave a shout. Books fell with a mighty sound. One of the books, a bright red "Worship the Lord" hymnal, stood out from the rest of the darker colored books. As soon as it fell, one child who had obviously listened well to the story of the spies in the land of Canaan, grabbed the hymnal, held it over his head, and happily shouted, "I've got Rahab!"

The class stopped. There was Garrett waving the red hymnal in the air, symbolic of salvation to the prostitute Rahab who had helped the Israeli spies and was told to put a scarlet cord in the window during the battle of Jericho so the troops could rescue her. Laughter erupted and ended the fall of Jericho, but the tableau of Garrett and "Rahab" will forever be in my mind.

The scarlet thread that saved Rahab and her family in the fall of Jericho is symbolic of the blood of Christ that can save all fallen people. Redemption came to one who was of the wrong race, the wrong gender, and, definitely, the wrong profession. Joshua, acting as God's representative, spared her life and changed history. Rahab was saved from certain death and elevated to a high position as one in the lineage of Christ himself. Genealogies in the Bible are seldom interesting to read, but the one in Matthew 1 should be cause for shouting! Rahab the harlot is now a revered entry in history.

Promise made.

Promise kept.

Required reading: *Salmon the father of Boaz, whose mother was Rahab, Boaz the father of Obed, whose mother was Ruth, Obed the father of Jesse, and Jesse the father of*

King David. [And 28 generations later…] *and Jacob the father of Joseph, the husband of Mary, to whom was born Jesus, who is called Christ. Matthew 1:5, 6, 16*

Homework: Think of the child in your class with the most confusing family tree, the one so entangled that it would be difficult to chart. The one whose birth certificate has "unknown" where the father's name belongs. Then remember that God may just have his hand on this child for a special place in history. Never judge by genealogy.

March

Mentors That Make a Difference

Every year our school hosts a Parent Appreciation Tea. Every year I have many names on the invitation list. There are so many people who have been volunteers in my room – parents, grandparents, PTA leaders, and even my own sweet husband and my mom and dad. The local high school even sends "PALS" to buoy up students needing a little extra encouragement. The school is always buzzing with volunteers running papers, laminating, cutting, and pasting. But there is a special group of volunteers known as mentors. These are people who have adopted a child or a class to love, teach, and shower with attention during the year. LaQuita, Kim, and Nancy are representative of that group of people who make a difference.

LaQuita was a multi-talented mother. She and her husband John were parents to two exceptionally wonderful sons. Listening in to one of LaQuita's small groups in my class, I realized how blessed these boys were to have her for a mom and how my little group would benefit from her expertise. She was teaching a lesson on the seasons and playing a seasons game. My note to her was probably brief and the materials handed to her quickly with few instructions. I heard her explaining to them interesting facts about the seasons and that they were opposite if you are in the southern hemisphere. She was extending the basic learning I had expected her to do.

She also taught her own sons to respect their teachers. She taught them by example. During Teacher Appreciation Week, she borrowed vans, recruited chauffeurs to drive and volunteers to watch our classes after lunch. Each grade level team was driven to her house during lunch for a gourmet meal, served on china by her willing group of PTA friends. We enjoyed a leisurely meal away from school. We really felt appreciated!

Kim had a small baby when she called the school to volunteer. She needed a break once a week and thought that this would be a way to give back to the community. She was sent to my room. Kim took to teaching like a duck to water. I would give her minimal notes to games to be played or lessons to be reviewed, and she would take off. She would work with any group or individual children. She helped the slower learners catch up and gave them extra attention. When she volunteered to come back for another year, and another, and another, I was delighted! One year I had a group of students who were very bright, but had not tested into the Talent Pool program. Feeling that these children needed more enrichment, I made special lesson plans for Kim to use with this group. Year after year she volunteered until, finally, Kim's baby boy was in my class! By then, other teachers and the PTA had found her. She began substituting and was a popular choice with both teachers and students. She has made lifelong friends in the school and is planning to get a teaching license when baby #2 is a little older.

Nancy's house backed up to the school. She had helped her husband and sons run a landscaping service. But, one day, on a walk past the school, feeling like she wanted to do more in life to help others, she went inside and volunteered. Her two sons had been in my class about 20 years before. The office called and asked if I remembered her. Instantly I did. They asked if I could use a helper. Of course, I could! Nancy would work with any group I assigned. One year I had a child in my class who should have been reading well, but she was not. I suspected that this child with the high IQ was having problems outside school that interfered with her progress. Nancy befriended Caroline, brought her small presents, encouraged her in reading, and we began to see signs of literacy. By the end of the year, Caroline was reading on second grade level.

Then one day I got a phone call at school. There were sobs on the other end. "Mrs. James, this is Christi, Nancy's daughter. My dad just passed away suddenly. Mom wanted me to call to let you know that she won't be in today."

"Oh, Christi," I said, "I am so sorry. Please tell your mom to take off as much time as she needs and not to worry about things here."

The funeral for the 52-year-old man was set for a few days later. Exactly one week after the funeral I got a call on the intercom. "Mrs. James, do you have some work for Mrs. Briskey to do? She would like to come in today."

Nancy came right over and said she had realized that the kids helped her more than she helped them. She continued to work with small groups and individual children until she moved out of state. She was always thinking of ways to make the whole class feel special – even those who didn't regularly work with her. She would bring small gifts to the entire class on holidays and was always so happy to see them. For her excellent mentoring, Nancy Briskey was honored by the North East Independent School District with the Spotlighter Award and her name appears on a brick on the walk of honor at the district offices.

God bless the mentors of the world – the unpaid, under-appreciated workers of inestimable worth.

Required reading: *Give and it will be given to you. A good measure, pressed down, shaken together and running over, will be poured into your lap. For with the measure you use, it will be measured to you.*
Luke 6:38

Homework: Give your mentors a gift and a note today saying, "You are appreciated! You are making a difference."

Extra credit reading: *We have different gifts, according to the grace given us. If a man's gift is…teaching, let him teach…Romans 12:6, 7*

Extra credit: Go volunteer yourself to teach Sunday School. If you think you can't teach on the weekend, you can! Try working with a different age group. You have a gift – use it!

It's a Texas Thang (But you might understand.)

Primary children often have difficulty with size and order. Texas children, in particular, have trouble with size and order of political borders. They cannot seem to understand the size of Texas in relation to the rest of the world. To try to help with this lesson, I found an old L'eggs egg, a large plastic Easter egg, a regular size Easter egg and a tiny plastic Easter egg. I labeled them in descending order: World, USA, Texas, San Antonio, and inside of the tiny plastic Easter egg I placed a tiny cutout house. The children could nest them over and over like babushka dolls.

This did not work.

So I cut a large red shape of the USA for every child. Onto this we glued smaller maps of Texas and onto Texas we glued even smaller replicas of the Alamo. On top of the Alamos, tiny white houses were glued, complete with their house numbers, if known. Some even drew themselves in the house.

This did not work either.

Most authorities would argue that primary children have limited perspective on size. I think it's a Texas "thang." Sort of like the King in *The King and I,* not believing that Siam was so small, Texas children cannot believe that there is more to the world than the Lone Star State. My friend Loyce, who knows a lot about such things, agrees. She even says that the Texas flag is the only state flag that, theoretically, could be carried at the same level with the US flag since Texas was once its own country for a brief period. Don't look for this to happen any time soon.

This "Texas is really big" attitude probably originates in the public school system that teaches bluebonnets, pecan trees, the Alamo, and mockingbirds in every grade of elementary school. It is possibly linked to the unique shape of the state, which can be used in the design of mouse pads, trivets, baskets, and even hot tubs.

In 2003, the state legislature determined that each child should say the Pledge to the Texas flag every day following the pledge to the US flag.

I once wrote the Texas pledge on the board so I could learn it since I am not a native.

"Honor the Texas flag. I pledge allegiance to Thee, Texas, one state under God, one and indivisible."

"Boys and girls, do you know what this is?" I asked.

Chris looked at it and hazarded a guess, "Is it the second verse of the Pledge of Allegiance?"

Spoken like a true Texan.

Required reading: *Therefore, it is necessary to submit to the authorities, not only because of possible punishment but*

also because of conscience. If [you owe] respect, then respect.
Romans 13:5

Homework: This week pay particular attention to posture and respect during the pledge, or pledges, if you live in Texas, and patriotic songs. Children have to be taught how to stop, stand at attention, remove hats, look at the flag, and speak the pledge in a respectful tone with hand on heart. Point out those who are particularly courteous.

Almost

Our son-in-law Scott is a great dad for his three young daughters. He compliments them, plays with them, teaches them, and loves each one for her unique personality. Since he loves sports, he once said, "I may have three girls, but they will all know how to throw a softball." Sure enough, when the girls were old enough, he signed them all up for softball teams.

Saddened that he had to miss one practice for his youngest daughter, he called six-year-old Brenna to him. "How did you do today in practice?" he asked.

"Good," smiled Brenna. "I had a lot of 'almost.' "

"What do you mean?" asked Scott.

"You know, when the coach says, 'Almost!'" she intoned in a benevolent coach-voice.

When I heard her say this, I had visions of "swing and a miss" as she stepped to the plate each time, but I admired her attitude. She tried, and tried, and came close!

All of us have "almosts" in our lives. We can see the cup "half-full" if we can learn to rejoice in our "almosts."

I was almost a child's favorite teacher once. Andre' really had a way with words. He wrote me that I was his "second favorite teacher." Let's see – kindergarten and first grade – two teachers. I just wish there could have been more entries in the contest!

My dad had told me a similar story of an "almost" in his life. He once won a third place ribbon in the long jump at his little country school. He said, "It would have had so much more meaning if there had been more than three boys in the competition."

Appreciating approximation comes in very handy when supervising first grade art project. Near Christmas I told the children that we were going to be doing a very hard art project. "But," I warned them, "I don't want any whining or anyone saying, 'I can't!'" I was about to begin the directions on how to fold the doilie to make an angel gown when James yelled out. "My mama always tells me, *'I can do all things through Christ who strengthens me.'*"

"Philippians 4:13 is a good scripture, James," I inserted as the Elmer's glue began to drip from angel wings. We were not all totally successful in making the heavenly hosts, but we were "almost!"

Fortunately, I had learned about approximation in a graduate psychology class. I had decided to try it out on our own baby boy who was nearing potty training age. My heady knowledge would have a practical use. Knowing Rick's penchant for candy-coated peanuts, I had an idea. I would reward him for approximation. Peanuts for nearing the bathroom. Peanuts for entering the bathroom. Peanuts for approaching the toilet. Peanuts for success. I was on a roll! Pavlov and his dog were right. I could probably write a book called *Potty Training with Peanuts.*

My visions of success were ignominiously shaken when I was cleaning house one day. I found a stray peanut and, out of habit, handed it to Rick. He took it and toddled into the bathroom to eat it. All that he had learned from my efforts was that we should eat peanuts in the bathroom. So much for approximation leading to potty training. Close, but no cigar. Or peanut.

Required reading: *As a father has compassion on his children, so the Lord has compassion on those who fear him for he knows how we are formed, he remembers that we are dust. Psalm 103:14*

Homework: Strive for, but don't expect, perfection from your "dusty" people. Be a good model of mistake making! Demonstrate by your life how we should keep trying even after we fail. "Almost" is the keyword.

Stick to the Subject

In my last year of teaching first grade before retirement, I asked for a student teacher, hoping to be able to give materials from decades of teaching to someone who might need them. What a worthy recipient I was assigned from Texas State University! Michelle Mesa (now Ramirez) came into my room and won my heart and the hearts of 20 first graders right away. Her ready smile and self-confidence made it very easy for me to turn over the class to her, one subject at a time.

One morning Michelle's lesson plans stated that she was going to work on writing on the topic. This is a big task in first grade. I once had a child who started writing about his brother and ended with a good story about Jose' Conseco and the rest of the Oakland A's baseball team.

After teaching a mini-lesson on "Sticking to the Subject," Michelle asked the children to work independently. One little boy was experiencing difficulty, apparent from a quiet pencil and a blank stare. Michelle quietly went to him and asked, "What do you want to write about, Michael?"

"The zoo."

"What do you want to tell about the zoo?"

"I'll get a snack there."

"What kind?"

"Popcorn."

"What will you see?"

"Eagles."

"Who will you go with?"

"My mom and my brother."

Gently, Michelle drew circles on a piece of paper and "webbed" all of his thoughts from a central circle named "Zoo." Then she left Michael to write his story. During the "Author's Chair" time, she affirmed Michael's hard work by asking him to read his story. He smiled and began,

"The Zoo.

I am going to the zoo.

I like the eagle.

I will have a snack.

It will be popcorn.

I will go with my mom and brother.

I love my family."

I was sitting at my desk in my advisory role, thinking, "Nab him, Michelle! Here is a great example of getting off the topic, talking about love of family in a zoo story." She read my mind and smiled back at me. There was a pause.

All at once, kind-hearted James spoke out, "Isn't that sweet?"

I was sitting at my desk in my advisory role, thinking, "Let it go, Michelle! 'Sweet' trumps 'subject' every time!" She wisely let it go, thanked Michael, and later had a good laugh with me at lunch about the blown opportunity that left a child's self-esteem intact.

Required reading: *"...do not exasperate your children; instead, bring them up in the training and instruction of the Lord." Ephesians 6:4*

Homework: Try the three cheers and a wish method of evaluating a child's writing. If another child (or the teacher) wants to be a critic, first give three cheers and then a make a wish. For example, to critique Michael's story, a friend could say that he liked the title, the fact that he wrote many words, and that he read in a loud voice. He could wish that Michael would write another story all about his family and how much he loves them.

April

Yelling Parents

Teachers can be guaranteed at least one yelling parent per school year. Why is that, you may ask? I think this is taught in Principalship 101, "You must spread out angry parents, so that every teacher can have one." Or, perhaps, it happens because you are the first teacher to tell them that their prodigy is not going to be attending Harvard. Or, more likely, it is because there are many hurting people in the world, and miserable people like to make others miserable. I had a friend who almost left teaching because of multiple encounters with a bipolar parent bent on ruining her career. My teacher-daughter tells of dealing with a lady who had multiple personalities. She says, "I never knew which one was coming to conference."

One of my pet peeves about these antagonistic parents is the fact that they like to send bad notes early in the morning. Here you come into a fresh room, ready to teach, only to be handed a note from the disgruntled parent telling you how wrong you are or what you need to be doing better. It takes real grace to not see their child in a bad light after receiving an angry note. One particular woman used to write me bad notes in CAPITAL LETTERS. It seemed that she was yelling at me on paper. Fortunately, colleagues can usually diffuse the hurt and help you see some humor in these mean-spirited letters.

It also helps to keep a file of kind letters from parents to help you be reminded that you have done a few good things in teaching children. Words of kindness are so very appreciated. "Would you consider teaching second grade next year? I'd love for him to have <u>you</u> again." Or "He really does love you. You have truly made him feel special. You welcomed him back when he needed you the most." God bless the parents who take the time to put good thoughts into words that we can hang on when we are being hammered by parents with a big ax to grind.

Required reading: *With the tongue we praise our Lord and Father, and with it we curse men, who have been made in God's likeness. Out of the same mouth come praise and cursing. My brothers, this should not be. James 3:9, 10*

Homework: Write a note to the teacher next door specifically commenting on how well she taught a certain lesson or handled a difficult conference. This note may come at the perfect time to lift up a teacher who has been stepped on. Our school had special "fish" cutout notes in a basket in the lounge so we could write messages of encouragement to put into other teachers' mailboxes. You could start this at your school.

Reality Shows

Reality shows are the surprise hits of the early 21st century. Who would have thought that so many people would tune in to watch people remodeling houses, getting a makeover, or just living their everyday lives? But children don't need to watch reality on TV. First graders <u>live</u> their own reality shows every day in the classroom. No holds barred. No doors shut. No sacred cows. And first grade has some pretty earthy moments.

Kenneth had a question for me. "Mrs. James, you never use the bathroom in our classroom. Do you go to the one in the building or do you just hold it all day?" Nothing is off-limits to a first grader.

A first grader's bluntness could possibly create problems. Our own first-grade granddaughter was chiding her mother for not knowing where to get information on how to tell the gender of baby rabbits that had just been born on their farm. "Mo-om," Annika patiently explained, "just go to the computer and type in <u>www.bunnybottoms.com</u>."

"Don't do it!" I warned my daughter as she told me of this conversation.

One day on my own reality series (that runs from August to May with no reruns), I was trying to teach map skills. Now there are certain subjects that first graders love to study. Among them are rocks, dirt, simple machines, and, believe it or not, map skills. They love learning that the compass points spell "NEWS." They love saying, "From the North, from the East, from the West, from the South, we bring you the NEWS." They love having a prize hidden in the room with following oral directions as the only means of finding it. "Go three steps North. Go two steps East. Go five more steps North." The whole class tingles as the uninformed child gets closer and closer to the prize. This game is a good one to fill tiny gaps in the schedule, but the children could play it nonstop.

With enthusiasm for map skills running high, it was a good day when we made our own individual maps of the room. Using circles, squares, and rectangles, we drew representations of our desks, chairs, computers, closets, and even the bathroom. Then I informed them that we were going to take our pencils on a "walk around the room" using our homemade maps. Happily, 20 pencils hopped onto their maps. I began the tour.

"Make the pencil come into the room." (Hop, hop, hop went the pencil men.)

"Make the pencil put up his backpack in the closet." (Hop, hop, hop.).

"Make the pencil go to your seat." (Hop, hop, hop.)

"Make the pencil go to the chalkboard." (Hop, hop, hop.)

"Make the pencil go into the bathroom." (Hop, hop, hop, Ssss.)

Reality show in first grade!

Having this bathroom right in our room is good for taking pencil men on walks. It is great for children who wait too long to go and have to make emergency landings. But a classroom bathroom has a few drawbacks due, in part, to the "If I can't hear you, then you can't hear me" syndrome. This condition is most notable among children using the bathroom or listening to a tape on headsets. Quite often a child will talk in a very loud voice while in the restroom or at the listening center.

One day Jeremy was in the bathroom at the back of the room. He was singing in a very loud voice. Unfortunately, it was during what we euphemistically call "Silent" Reading. This misnomer actually means that you read only to yourself. It's not really silent. I sent Rafael to ask him to be quieter in the bathroom. This did not help. When Jeremy finally emerged, I called him to me and said, "Jeremy, I could hear you way up here. You were singing in the bathroom."

In a very self-righteous voice, wanting to justify himself, he argued, "I was singin' <u>and</u> poopin'!" That was more reality than I needed.

Required reading: *Speak to one another with psalms, hymns and spiritual songs. Sing and make music in your heart to the Lord, always giving thanks to God the Father for everything, in the name of our Lord Jesus Christ. Ephesians 5:19, 20*

Homework: Kids are unrefined creatures. They need to be taught to tell the truth. They also need to learn how much information is appropriate in a school setting.

The Veil in the Temple

Our junior class at Sunday School had been studying the Old Testament stories about the tabernacle. We had a small model of it in the classroom, but my husband and I thought a lifesize model would be much more effective. We measured the church gym and were delighted that it would be a fairly close representation of the size of the tabernacle. It even faced east/west as the tabernacle did. We planned an all-day Saturday play/project time. After some pizza, we began to let our imaginations run wild.

The pool table would be about the right size for the "Altar of Burnt Offering."

Red and yellow tissue paper could be crumpled to become the perpetual flames on the altar.

A poster board cut-out of a lamb could be the sacrifice.

A big bowl could be the "Laver" for the "priests" to wash their hands.

A volleyball net was hung with assorted tablecloths and sheets to separate the "Holy Place" from the "Holy of Holies."

We got to work on the "Holy Place." Plastic banks that looked like loaves of bread were leftover from a missionary offering campaign were perfect for the "Bread of the Presence." We found 12 little banks to put on the "Table of Shewbread." The "Candlestick" was easy to replicate as one of the parents had a gold candlestick with the seven candles on top. The "Altar of Incense" was placed right in front of the curtain separating the two parts of the tabernacle.

Working on the Ark of the Covenant for the "Holy of Holies" was a challenge. Fortunately, we had brought some large cardboard boxes. We spray-painted a large box gold for the "Ark of the Covenant." We got to use our math and art skills to draw and cut out two angels with their wings touching over the top. Inside the ark we placed "Manna" (Quaker's Oats), the 10 Commandments written on two cardboard tablets, and Aaron's rod that bloomed (a mop handle with silk lilies taped to it.)

When we were confident that the tabernacle was ready, and the "Israelites" had time for more pizza and play, we began to assign parts. We raided the church's limited costume supply to make us look somewhat authentic. One student was to be an Israelite bringing the paper lamb to be sacrificed. Others were placed at strategic points in the gym as guides, and we began to practice for a "Tabernacle Tour."

On Sunday morning it was announced that the adults were invited to attend the tour that evening at 6 p.m. At sunset our guests began arriving. We walked the visitors into the gym to the pool table altar and demonstrated the laver and the sacrificial lamb. Next they visited the "Holy Place" where the different guides told them about the "Candlestick," the "Altar of Incense," and the "Table of Shewbread."

Then the group walked toward the sheets and tablecloths closing off the "Holy of Holies." Sarah, the student in charge of this part of the tour, explained the enormous significance of this most sacred place. With great drama she parted the "curtain," and asked the group to step inside for the rest of the tour. I stepped into the "Holy of Holies" and was overtaken at that moment with a sense of quiet awe. Sarah had demonstrated what God did for us just as Jesus was dying on the cross. He ripped the veil that separated God and man and forever let us have access to God. No longer was this place so restricted that a priest may have had a string tied to his leg so he could be pulled out of this place in case of his death. Now everyone has the power to enter this most holy place of communion with God freely. I have always loved the King James wording of what happened during the crucifixion. The curtain was "rent in twain from the top to the bottom," an ancient way of saying the veil was ripped in two by God Himself from heaven to earth. The visual of the makeshift tabernacle and the junior-size guides will remain as one of my most precious memories ever.

Required reading: *The curtain of the temple was torn in two from top to bottom. Mark 15:38*

For we do not have a High Priest who is unable to sympathize with our weaknesses, but we have one who has been tempted in every way just as we are, yet was without sin. Let us then approach the throne of grace with confidence, so that we may receive mercy and find grace to help us in our time of need. Hebrews 4:15, 16

Homework: Take full advantage of the ripped veil! Bring all of your teaching problems and personal problems to the One who is waiting for you to step on into the Holy of Holies and talk to Him.

Laughing All the Way

When I began teaching first grade, I also began working with a team of teachers with the rather bland title of "First Grade Team." This team became a very large part of my life for the 27 years that I was privileged to work with this dedicated group of professionals. The personnel changed over the years, but the camaraderie and closeness did not change. Even in times of discouragement, we had each other. Elspeth Campbell Murphy wrote about this in *Chalkdust*, a book of prayers especially for teachers.

> "Oh, but it was exhilarating
> out on the playground this morning, Father.
> Exhilarating,
> to put our petty differences aside,
> join our hands and hearts,
> and raise our voices
> in One Great Gripe.
> The exhilarating unity!
> The spirit of camaraderie!
> The fun of the common cause!
> It's the stuff of revolution! *

More often than not, however, laughter, not the "Great Gripe" has helped us through difficult conferences, uncomplimentary notes from parents, or life situations outside of school. We have come through pregnancies, child-rearing, graduations, cancer, retirements, in-laws, and deaths. We have been a closely-knit group. We have had Christmas parties together, prayed together, and cheered together at football games. We have huge birthday parties for each other, or even unbirthdays for those of us born in the summer. These celebrations have enough food for at least two days, colorful table settings, and many gifts and cards.

One summer the first grade team decided to plan "Teacher Field Trips." We thought of places that teachers would like to go – to the Promised Land Dairy with no children to corral, shopping at the Outlet Mall in San Marcos without having to keep people in line. No money was collected; no advance notice was needed to join the fun. We just printed a list of fun places that we were going and the date and opened it to the entire faculty. We met in the school parking lot to carpool.

Our staff also was able to have a very "San Antonio" Christmas a couple of years as we were invited to carol under the sparkling colored lights on the San Antonio River on a river barge. These times of fun outside of school cements the faculty bond and makes coming to work even more enjoyable.

I recently made a speech to the graduating teachers at the University of Texas at San Antonio. In the speech I made a statement, praising our school and team, stating that I wished everyone could work in such a wonderful school. Shortly after this, our principal went to a job fair and was inundated by new teachers wanting to join the El

Dorado faculty. Who wouldn't want to work in a sharing, loving community?

I was inducted into the humor of this group my very first week on the job. All of the first grade teachers brought classes to the playground at the same time to learn the rules so we would all be on the same page since we shared recess duty. My new friend Sally addressed the huge group of children eager to get on with play and teachers relieved that Sally was the spokesperson. One of our rules was "No rock throwing." Sally painted a bleak verbal picture of what the consequences could be for breaking this rule. "I know a man who had a rock thrown at him in first grade. He is now a 30 year-old-man and has no front teeth." I don't know why but that struck my funny bone. I could just imagine a man who had gone for 24 years and never done anything about his dental problem. Laughter welled up in my belly. I wanted to laugh so badly. I wanted to cackle. I really had to exert self-control to keep from ruining the safety speech. Welcome to first grade!

Another year several of us met spontaneously after school and decided to practice the new science program. It was a huge DVD with mostly still pictures to be narrated by the teacher. Without getting out the teacher's guide, our informal group decided to do our own dialogue. Witty Barbara started it, and the group became hysterical. Never had first grade science been so entertaining. We laughed so hard at our own cleverness with our ad-lib science lesson. Then, weak with laughter, we began to wonder why Janine hadn't joined us. She was just two rooms down. Surely she could hear her delirious cohorts. We went to her classroom and found her with her head on her desk, fast asleep. Sometimes first grade just wears a person down.

Janine had her day to narrate later. We had accidentally ordered a social studies video in Spanish. Janine and I tried our best to interpret, using our high school Spanish. It was a debacle. Monica, one of Janine's students, stepped up and translated beautifully. (No entendemos español muy bien.)

New teachers are welcomed at our school from day one – and sometimes before. Our team liked to go shopping or have a carry-in lunch to get to know new team members. That way, by the time we went to inservices, we were already a team.

Kelley was a new teacher to our school, transferring from another local elementary. Our team and the new speech teacher had all gone to Taco Cabana for Mexican food after a morning inservice. Laughter, talking and eating were in high gear as the group became better acquainted. But suddenly, and without warning, a break amazingly came in the conversation, just in time to hear Kelley speaking on her cell phone. "Did my wand come in?" she was saying. The crowded patio restaurant rocked with laughter! We were all wondering what royalty had come to grace our team. She tried to regain her composure in order to finish the conversation. We all strained to hear. "OK, just leave it at the dry cleaners, and I'll pick it up later." Now we were definitely gone! We had just hired a princess who dry-cleaned her wand! Now we had tears streaming down our faces.

For the record – Kelley had ordered a wand from her dentist. She was going to use it in her class. The dentist's office was closing before she could pick it up, so they were going to leave it next door at the cleaners. Does that clear it up?

Kelley has never recovered from the wand incident. She has received princess cards, a lighted wand and sparkles for her hair, and her story has gone down in the folklore annals of El Dorado Elementary.

Friends, compadres, confidants, companions – definitely more than just employees who happen to work together.

Required reading: *A friend loves at all times, and a brother is born for adversity. Proverbs 17:17*

My command is this: Love each other as I have loved you. John 15:12

Homework: Plan a shopping trip or a teacher-only field trip to get to know your teaching buddies better. Or, better yet, get a group (two or three is fine) to meet once a week to pray for the protection and effectiveness of your school and for the needs of individual teachers. Meet after hours in a classroom. We did!

Chalkdust by Elspeth Campbell Murphy, Baker Book House, p. 43

May

Little Mans

We have a trophy case in our home with trophies of every size and description. There are golden people celebrating journalism, youth camp, riflery, beauty, baseball, football, track, soccer, and even one with a car perched on top. Our son won a driver's education trophy when he was in high school. Do you know how hard it is to be a parent trying to correct the driving of a 16-year-old boy who owns a driver's ed trophy? Any suggestion of mine concerning his driving was met with, "Uh, uh, uh, who has the trophy?"

Sadly, none of the golden people is mine. They all belong to my husband, daughter, and son. But I do have one great talent to my credit. Over the years I have become quite adept at predicting which of the children in my class might actually win sports trophies. I didn't get the nickname "Jock Mama" for nothing.

One year I had a very low reading class. To help their reading ability and to put some life into a story with limited vocabulary, I proposed doing a play. We got our little books, decided on parts, gathered props, and began. One little curly-headed boy laboriously read, " I can jump. See me jump, jump, jump!" Then the tiny blond child stood and did one of the best standing broad jumps I have ever seen. I was amazed. I could see five colored Olympic circles linked above him as he made his way to the platform to accept the gold medal in a few short years, tearfully thanking the first grade teacher who discovered his talent. I had him do a few more jumps on the playground that day just to make sure it wasn't a fluke. It wasn't.

Now I was on a mission. I called his mom, a single parent and begged her to let him enter the San Antonio summer games. She said she had to work nights. Undaunted, I told her that I would take him home to his grandmother if she would just get him to the stadium.

I was sitting in the stands when his mom arrived with Danny in tow. Unfortunately, she had to leave before seeing him on the winner's stand with a bronze medal around his neck. I snapped photos like a proud parent and later drove him home to a grandmother who had also missed all of the fun. I lost track of my broad jumper when he moved away from our school. But, hopefully, his moment of glory provided a great memory for him.

Another of my students was tall and athletic. Predicting the future, I told him one day, "Travis, you will play ball for Madison (local high school) someday, and I'm coming to see you."

"Oh, I don't think so," he said, doubting my words.

"Why not?"

He sized up my already gray hair and said, "You'll be too old."

"Travis," I corrected him, "if I have to come in a wheelchair to see you, I'll be there!"

Years later Travis was indeed a starting varsity basketball player at James Madison High School. I walked into the fieldhouse under my own power. I made sure his parents saw me, so they could tell Travis that I was there, unassisted. Years later Travis showed up at my retirement party, a tall and handsome man, and probably saying to himself, "She's got to be really old now - and she still gets around!"

Over the years I have been able to see many of my former students compete in sports, one of the joys of staying in the same area for a very long time.

A friend from Mexico who was just learning English was admiring our trophy case one day and told our son, "I like your little mans."

I later told Rick, "That's what they are – just little mans, and unless you have grown from the experiences that earned the little mans, they don't matter much."

I love the old hymn "The Old Rugged Cross" by George Bennard.

> "So I'll cherish the old rugged cross,
> 'Til my trophies at last I lay down;
> I will cling to the old rugged cross,
> And exchange it someday for a crown."

I don't know if Mr. Bennard had "little mans" in 1913 or not, but he seems to know that all of our earthly signs of athletic prowess, wealth, and intelligence will one day bow to a returning Savior.

Required reading: *Have nothing to do with godless myths and old wives' tales; rather, train yourself to be godly. For physical training is of some value, but godliness has value for all things, holding promise for both the present life and the life to come. I Timothy 4:7, 8*

Therefore God exalted him to the highest place and gave him the name that is above every name, that at the name of Jesus every knee should bow, in heaven and on earth, and under the earth and every tongue confess that Jesus Christ is Lord to the glory of God the Father. Philippians 2:9-11

Homework: Watch for signs of gifts and intelligences other than academic. Praise children for aptitude in social skills, virtues, mechanical ability, or athletics.

Gifts

Elementary teachers often receive gifts that are childlike. Our gift-picker-outers choose gifts that they would like to receive. Consequently, we get many stuffed animals, particularly bears, coffee mugs, particularly those with bears on them, and many apple (or bear) knick-knacks. I have acquired enough apple decorations to help embellish a kitchen. Teachers occasionally still get real apples like in the olden days. One of the most unusual gifts I have received was a real 7-Up bottle, emptied of soda and filled with bath salts. Another time a child came in with a handful of flavored coffee packets. "We had too many, so Mom said I could bring you some," was the explanation.

Joe Alex, upon hearing of my upcoming retirement, wanted to give me a gift. "Mrs. James, you don't have a pet, do you?"

"No, I used to, but my dog Fletcher died."

"Well, I am thinking of getting you a pet."

"What kind of pet?"

"I'm thinking a rooster or a chicken."

This would be a memorable gift. I have had a chicken as a pet before, but never a rooster.

First graders love to make gifts for their moms and dads. They also love to make original Christmas, Valentine's Day, Get Well or Mother's Day cards. One of the most memorable Mother's Day cards was from Don, the youngest of three children in his family. He wrote, (sic) "I love it when you were your flower niht gown. I oh so like it when we cutul. When I am big I will still love you. It will be hord when I get mered." What a gift of love. I think even his wife will be understanding after they are "mered."

The best Mother's Day gift I ever received was from my middle-school daughter. It was a polyester/cotton blend dress with pink flowers. The waist was hand-sewn and the hemline was a little lopsided. She decided to make it three days before Mother's Day. Her home economics teacher said it couldn't be done. That was like saying, "Sick 'em" to a dog. Julie was going to finish it and prove her wrong. I was touched as the procession began on Sunday - first the cards, then breakfast in bed, and then The Dress. Of course, I wore it to church proudly on that Sunday, and I still have it a quarter of a century later.

Required reading: *When he ascended on high he led captives in his train and gave gifts to men. Ephesians 4:8b*

Homework: One of the best gifts to give parents is a picture of their child on the first day of school. Dressed in their best with a little apprehension in their smiles, they make a charming picture. Save the pictures and put inside a homemade Christmas card or Mother's Day card.

Teachers Never Really Lose Their Class

One of my favorite lines from children's literature is one that is not really understood by the children when I read it. It comes from *Teach Us, Amelia Bedelia* by Peggy Parish. In the story, Mr. and Mrs. Rogers go to the airport to pick up the new teacher. Amelia Bedelia goes to the school to tell them that the plane is late. She is mistaken for the new teacher and has to teach all day. There are many misadventures because of her inability to understand idioms or double meanings. When the real teacher arrives, the children are gone, and Mrs. Rogers quizzes Amelia Bedelia.

"Where are the children?"

"Home," said Amelia Bedelia.

"But it's not time," said Mrs. Rogers.

"It was for me," said Amelia Bedelia.

This bit of educational humor goes right over the heads of first graders. They can't fathom that a teacher might need a rest. They are not even aware that teaching is a job. One child asked me, "Do you work somewhere?" I'm always amused that, when we study antonyms, the children do very well until we get to the opposite of "play."

That stumps them. I guess that is because so much of our "work" is "play" that the dichotomy is not apparent.

I have tried at times to lose my class. One day I walked quickly into the cafeteria for lunch, turned around, and found no children behind me. My long legs had gone too fast for their little ones. But that was only a temporary loss. Teachers can never really lose their class.

You can send them home at 2:45, but they are still in your head - sometimes into the middle of the night! You try to go home to cook supper and find yourself recycling the trash for art projects. You can try to shop for groceries, but you will find stickers and glitter and markers for your class. Your conversation with total strangers is about the funny things that happened in class that day. You can't go home by yourself.

You can hug them goodbye for the summer, but they'll come back the next year. They will write you notes from the next grade. I had one child who had raised enough Cain in my class to live in the folklore of El Dorado Elementary for years. Everyone knew him. He was like Cher, Pele, Shaq – his first name was all you needed! It would drum up visions of disrupted lessons, office referrals, and insolent looks. He had more letters after his name than a PhD. He was LD, ADD, ADHD, ODD and my own diagnosis SI (Socially Ineffective.) Right before school was out for the summer, I got a note from him. [sic] "I will mihs you and i will come to your cashrom next year. Love by Max" This semi-threatening message did come true. He did come to see me often – with hugs, even.

You can send them off to middle school, high school, or even to college. Some of your students will <u>drive</u> back to see you. Then you begin to get invitations – to graduations, weddings, and later, even to bridal and baby showers. Some even bring their children back to the classroom to see you.

You can move or retire, but you can't really lose your class. You will still be on the pages of college essays about influential people in their lives. You will still be a subject of conversation at family reunions when relatives tell them what funny things they did in first grade. You will still receive cards, letters, and e-mails from grateful students and parents who swear that you were almost part of their family. Actually, you were. It is a scary thought to think of the influence a teacher has, not just on the individual student, but on the entire family.

One of my most treasured e-mails was a note from a very quiet student who had been in my class about 20 years before. James is now a Border Patrol in South Texas. He had found my name on the Internet and just wanted to say thanks. He said he had the phone number of a high school teacher on his desk that he had intended to call to express appreciation for his teaching. Unfortunately, the man had passed away before James got to call. James didn't want that to happen again. He was contacting teachers in his life who had made a difference. He wrote, "I think my positive outlook on life and desire to succeed began in your classroom." He told many of his memories of the class he had been in 20 years earlier.

One of the most touching notes I have is from a former math student who is now teaching first grade herself. She wrote to me after reading my first book, *I Love Monday Mornings*. "I was encouraged by your book because being called to the ministry of teaching is tough.

Now that I am in it, and this is only my third year, I sometimes question myself. Am I patient enough? Do I have enough love? Can I physically make it through the strains of the day? And then be so disheartened by upset parents, or non-supportive parents, or meanness in kids, as well as disrespect. Sometimes I feel that I am not making a difference in their little lives. Your book has reminded me that I can." Jaime Elam Bailey

Primary teachers cast a long shadow. And teachers never really lose their class!

Required reading: *Not many of you should presume to be teachers, my brothers, because you know that we who teach will be judged more strictly. James 3:1*

Homework: Keep a file with students' names, addresses, and phone numbers. Also keep a copy of the class picture every year. You will need them for future reference.

Extra credit: If you are young enough, contact one of your "old" teachers who made a difference. It will really lift their spirits.

Walking Backwards

There is so much about the human brain that we do not know. In fact, brain research may be the new frontier in the 21st century. Perhaps some student in your class today will be on the scientific team to find a cure for brain cancer, Alzheimer's, Parkinson's disease, or other maladies of the brain. First graders know a couple of things about the brain now. Kyle once told me at the end of a busy morning, "My stomach is empty, but my brain is full."

Allen explained how he knew that 9-2=7. "I just walk backwards in my brain."

So, students can understand that a brain can get full and that you can walk backwards in your brain. Sometimes teachers need to understand these two facts, too.

Your brain can get full of all of the mistakes you have made. You have not demonstrated the Fruit of the Spirit. You said the wrong thing at faculty meeting. You forgot a report that was due. You offended a parent. You used sarcasm on a child. You have blown it! We all have! There is not a teacher alive who has not transgressed against a child, his parent, or another teacher! Even when you have been forgiven by God and by the offended party, it is sometimes hard to self-forgive.

I often regain perspective on forgiveness by watching a little Spurs basketball, OK, a lot of Spurs basketball! I've seen these very highly paid professionals put up air balls, lose the player they were supposed to guard, or completely blow a slam-dunk. If those athletes beat themselves up mentally, they couldn't possibly get back down the court, let alone win championships! Self-forgiveness must be done almost instantly in order to get on with the game.

One way to help exonerate yourself is to say, "That's not like me." And then go on!

Teachers who have experienced the forgiveness of God through His son Jesus know the "made new" feeling of forgiveness. The ancient words of John 3:16 are still the best. *"For God so loved the world that he gave his one and only Son, that whoever believes in him shall not perish but have eternal life." But read on…John 3:17 begins, "For God did not send his Son into the world to condemn the world…"* God does not want you to be condemned. Not by Him, not by others, not by yourself. You <u>can</u> walk backwards in your brain and be forgiven.

After forgiveness has been proffered, remind God of your mess-up. He will say, "What sin?" And if He doesn't remember it, neither should you.

Required reading: *For I will forgive their wickedness and will remember their sins no more.*
Hebrews 8:12

Homework: Let it go!